WA H OF GREATNESS

Living an Extraordinary Life of Purpose, Impact, and Influence

S.G LIBS

WALKING THE PATH OF GREATNESS

www.sterlinglibs.com

London, United Kingdom

Editions ISBNs

Paperback: 9781911037279

"It always seems impossible until it's done"
Nelson Mandela

So, go, make your life a masterpiece. Tap into your potential. Do something extraordinary. Follow your dreams. Live your life the best way you can.
Be Great.

TABLE OF CONTENTS

Note to the Reader

Ever heard of the phrase – "*Knowledge is Power*"? I believe that there is more to it than just that. I believe that knowledge is only potential power, and it is what you do with it that will unleash that power and effect great things in your life.

This book comes your way loaded with that potential power and it is up to you what you will do with it. If you want to see great change and transformation in your life, my recommendation is that you be a doer, and not just a reader or listener to what is contained herein. My hope is that you will do your best to enrich your life many, many times over as a result of the insights and secrets you'll glean and apply from this book.

I have made every effort to make this book as complete and accurate as possible. However, I encourage you to be open minded and independent in your thinking to get the most out of it. Read it with a curious and inquisitive mind.

I pass the information herein to you with the understanding that neither my publisher nor I, are engaged in rendering any accounting, legal, or any other professional advice, and if you need any of those expert services, please seek the help of a competent professional.

Finally, if you do find any mistakes that might have slipped my scrutiny while finalising this book, do be gracious to my oversight, and I hope you'll still enjoy the book.

INTRODUCTION

I am Sterling Libs. I believe that one of the most valuable gifts you can give yourself is Time. Time to make the most of your life; Time to be the best you can be; Time to be authentically true to yourself. Being true to yourself is all about having the courage to live out your own unique Greatness, and I wrote this book to give you a road map – a road map to walking that Path of Greatness that is uniquely yours and not a copy. The 22 ways for doing so, explained in this book in the form of principles, insights, and secrets have been used by millions of people all over the world to transform their lives in extraordinary ways, enabling them to unleash their personal power and realise their personal freedom, and I hope that that will be your story and experience too.

I came to London England as a student many, many years ago. I was single, timid, afraid, and broke. Fast forward to today, and thanks to the insights and principles in this book, I am now happily married with four children, I am an entrepreneur running two very successful businesses. I am no longer timid or shy, but bold, decisive, confident, courageous, and yes, doing relatively well financially too. I delight in Wisdom, I work hard, and walk my own path of Greatness. I discovered that you can have whatever you want in life if you have the courage to follow your dreams and persist.

This book project took over ten years to complete, and it has been a terrific journey. I believe your journey to becoming more inspired and emboldened to live an authentic and successful life, starts right now. Read, and re-read this book again and again, and recommend it to your friends and family too. The insights and revelations contained in it have the potential to enormously help you to masterfully and gallantly live an extraordinary life of purpose, impact and influence, every day.

Peace and Love, *carpe diem* - **Sterling Libs.**

1

TAKING BACK CONTROL OF YOUR LIFE AND COMMANDING YOUR DESTINY

"It's been said that the gate of history turns on small hinges, and so do people's lives. The choices we make determine our destiny".
Thomas S Monson

Your life is your own to live, and ultimately, you are responsible for how it turns out. There is greatness in each of us, but few there be that realise it in their lifetime here on earth.

Through the information in this book, you have the opportunity to start walking the path of greatness unique to you.

Here is the thing, realising your greatness, and living the kind of life you want to live depends a great deal on whether or not you are truly in charge or in control of your life. It's really that simple.

Here then is a question I have for you; Who is it that is calling the shots in your life? Who is in charge? Is it you, or is it somebody or something else?

If not you, then whom have you relinquished your personal power to? Who is running the show in your life? Is it the debts you have? Is it fear? Is it your spouse? Children? Parents? In-laws? Or is it peoples' opinions? Or the News media? Do you know who it is?

Look, if you are not in control of your life, someone else or something else is. Period.

So, you have a decision to make right now, and it is this: Are you going to be a victim in life or a master of your destiny in life? It is a mutually exclusive decision that only you can and have to make. If the kind of life you are living currently is not the one you ideally want, the onus is on you to go after the kind you want to live.

If you know that there is something better out there for you, something you desire, something different, perhaps you want more say in the things that matter to you, or more freedom to decide how things should be done in your life, or it may be that you want to earn more money, or to have better and more meaningful relationships. Whatever it is you want, I hope you are not planning on wasting any more time cowering or being afraid or having self-pity, but rather are geared up and ready to start taking action to get on with designing and taking charge of your life and destiny and unleash the greatness within you.

Now would be the ideal time to stop pretending that everything is okay when it isn't. Now would be the time to acknowledge that something needs to be done. Now would be the time to gather the courage to be true to yourself and stop pretending to be somebody you're not or try to please everybody in order to fit in or be accepted by others. Now would be the time to take back control of your life and destiny and start following your dreams. Now would be the time to unleash your personal power and realise your personal freedom.

This is what this book is all about. And over its next few chapters, you will find some great, time-tested principles, and insights you can use to enormously help you realise your personal power and freedom to be who you want to be or do what you want to do to walk the path of greatness in your life.

The thing is, the responsibility for transforming your life from what it is right now to what you want it to be, is yours and yours alone, and you should not neglect or ignore to take up that responsibility, and neither should you delegate it.

To effect lasting changes in your life requires a total commitment to living your life with audacity, mustering the courage to authentically be true to yourself and follow your dreams. No if's, no but's. Total and unreserved audacious commitment. And I know for a fact that there is a lot you can accomplish in life if you are committed, and confident in your ability to make a success of it.

The reality though is that most people are not that much committed to their own sense of being and success, and thus are not walking the path of greatness. Some are aware of this, others are not.

Whether consciously or unconsciously, when you let someone else or something else be in control of your life and destiny, it is much to your detriment and sorrow than your joy. Don't let that be your story. Take an active and proactive role in running your own life instead of being a passive player in it, one who relinquishes control to others, and suffers the consequences of doing so.

Now, let me show you how you can arrive to that point in your life where you are fully in charge, and living a life of freedom, happiness, and having the personal power to control and command your life and destiny. A point where you tell your life story and tell it your way, walking your own path of greatness.

However, if you are wondering whether it is possible to be fully in control of your life and destiny, given perhaps what you might have been through in life so far, my answer to you would be, yes, it is possible. I have done it, and so too have many people who overcame the odds to champion the course of their own lives. And I believe you too, can do it, and here is how:

Are you ready? Let's go.

To begin with, start by renewing your mind, and taking full responsibility for your decisions and actions, and stop blaming other people for things you don't like about your life.

Take 100% responsibility for everything that you experience in your life. This includes the level of your achievements, the results you produce, the quality of your relationships, the state of your health and physical fitness, your income, your debts, your feelings, everything! All of that should be your responsibility.

You know what? You have the power to make a difference in your life, the power to get things right, and to produce the results you desire in your life. Yes, you do. Choose to exercise that power and draw a line from today on the past. Yes, the past is the past, and all that matters now is that from this point forward, you choose—that's right, it's a choice—you choose to be 100% responsible for everything that defines your experience of life. Stop giving excuses for your failures and mishaps and stop accepting excuses from others either, excuses for their lacklustre performances and behaviour. Be the man or woman who gets things done and get rid of lazy and incompetent people from your life by first getting the laziness and incompetence out of your own life.

I also want you to remember that when you embark on this journey of being fully in charge and engaged in the affairs of your life, and not being passive in it, there may be bumps along the way, and not everything might go your way initially. You may have to make some adjustments as you go along, but in the end, taking charge of your life, is a noble thing to do. However, you must also make sure that you take care not to interfere with the lives of other people. That is, let others have their own perfect liberty (such as you, yourself, exercise), to choose their own opinions, and way of life. It is after all, a free world we live in, isn't it? Don't seek to control others, let them be, just as you want to be let be.

That is the first thing you should do – take full responsibility for the outcomes in your life. Hold yourself accountable. No excuses anymore, the buck stops with you. Be in charge. Be in control. Make that call.

Secondly, you need to master your **Desires, your Beliefs, and your Fears.**

The truth is, human desires are vast, and people's beliefs range from the simple to the ridiculous, and their fears are numerous. And unless you step in and master your desires, beliefs, and fears, you run the risk of being tossed here and there, and often feeling out of control and helpless.

Let us begin by considering mastery of your **Desires.**
You see, your desires are part of you, and though you cannot stop yourself from desiring, you can, however, decide what to do with your desires. The thing is, human desires are vast, and they drive human behaviour. And if left unchecked, they have the potential to cause some serious problems.

When it comes to desires, they either have to be expressed or transmuted. I would caution you against suppressing or repressing your desires purely based on say, religious dogmas, beliefs, or unquestioned assumptions. Doing so, won't really work. And here is why; you see, desires, when suppressed or repressed, won't just disappear into thin air, no, they won't. They will try to find outlets to express themselves in you however much you try to suppress them. They will basically keep coming back in a disguised manner, and soon or later, you will find yourself indulging in them. And depending on the nature of those desires, you will have to reckon with the consequences or outcomes thereof.

If the desires you have are noble, they should be pursued and expressed, but if they are ignoble and selfish, they should be acknowledged, and then transmuted to more nobler ends. But what you should not do is suppress them. Some people have actually suffered mental and psychological problems because of suppressed or repressed desires. Don't let that happen to you too.

In dealing with my desires for example, I've found that it is more beneficial to filter them through the golden rule (this one - *do to others what you would have them do to you*) and with that, I infuse my desires with Love. For me, it is about holding and cultivating those desires that do me, and my fellow human beings' good, and no harm. It is also about being rational with my irrational desires, that is, I reason with myself about those irrational desires, and I try to be objective in doing so. It is not always easy, and I sometimes falter and fall, but I keep getting up until I win, and I believe you can too. Follow the golden rule in dealing with your desires.

Let's consider **mastery of your Beliefs**, next.

The truth is, beliefs, and unquestioned dogmas that you willingly submit yourself to, are very, very powerful, and they can hold you hostage for a very, very long time if you follow them blindly. Consequently, it increasingly becomes difficult for you to be in charge of your life under those circumstances because the beliefs are sort of in charge and running the show in your life.

That's why years ago, I decided to start reviewing my beliefs with an open mind and be willing to get rid of any beliefs that were not helping me advance in my life. Of course, I made it sacrosanct to abide by the golden rule whenever I was evaluating or re-evaluating my beliefs, and I still do.

Paul said in his 1st letter to the Thessalonians chapter five, verse 21 and 22 that; "*Test all things; hold fast what is good. Abstain from every form of evil.*"

So, for me, I don't blindly follow or imbibe ideas and beliefs or prophecies. No, I test them out.

Have I in the past been held hostage by erroneous beliefs?

O Yes, you bet I have, many, many times.

Did I change my mind when I realised that what I was believing was flawed?

O Yes, I did.

And was it hard? Hard to change my mind?

Initially, yes. You see, it is not that easy to disentangle yourself from something that has almost become part of you after many, many years of repeated use and exposure to it. However, with experience, over time, it becomes easy to separate yourself from false and ideological beliefs as you grow more in self-confidence and understanding of the nature of things.

Here is the thing, your beliefs influence a great deal of your life and in fact, sort of run your life. And so, it makes sense to evaluate them from time to time and ditch the ones that are unnecessarily holding you back. Learn to challenge your beliefs from time to time.

I know for a fact that what many people are taught in their childhood, and the experiences they go through growing up, come to form a big part of their belief system later in life. However, just because you were taught, or experienced certain things in your childhood and in your youth, does not necessarily mean that all those things still hold true today.

On the other hand, for some people, because of some bad experiences they have had in relationships, many of them, inadvertently go on to form some very unhelpful beliefs that then start affecting their lives negatively.

Now, look, your beliefs are a myriad of all sorts of things, some reasonable, and some totally weird. So, you've got to thoroughly test your beliefs, and challenge them. Test them to see whether they have any validity in your life now, today, in this day and age. Make sure you choose to hold beliefs that empower you to live a fuller life, and not a mediocre and self-defeating one. It is with your beliefs that you give meaning to life, and your beliefs also form the core foundation of the support structures of your life.

So, be careful what you chose to believe. Stand guard at the door of your mind and be strict about what you let into your mind and life.
I recommend that you take an audit of your beliefs right now, ask yourself where you got them from, and whether they are supporting you in living your life the way you want to, within reason and Love. Ask whether those beliefs are helping you to be in charge of your life or not, and then do the appropriate thing. Will you do that? I hope you will.

Moving on, I have so far talked about desires, and beliefs, and would now like to move on and talk about fear, because, taking charge of your life, and following your dreams, living the way you want to, is also dependent, to a large extent, on whether or not you allow fear to dominate your thinking.

Fear can be very disempowering and disheartening, and if you have ever faced fears of any sort, I trust you know exactly what I am talking about here.

Now, according to the online dictionary, fear is defined as *an unpleasant emotion caused by the threat of danger, pain, or harm.*

And you know what? Fear is normal. You see, given the fact that the desire for self-preservation is innate, fear, in a way is a sort of natural gravitation to that desire. When the threat of the danger, pain, or harm is imminent, experiencing fear at that time is normal. What is not normal, however, is to let fear dominate you. Even worse, is the tendency to magnify the fear, which unfortunately many of us tend to do.

To be honest, you can never be confidently in charge of your life, or successfully pursue your dreams, if you let fear, of any sort, dominate you.

So, how do you deal with fear and not let it control your life, so to say? How do you do that?

First of all, you need to realise that to be afraid is perfectly normal and expected because of your innate desire to preserve your life, and interests, from any threats of danger, pain, loss, or harm. If you see a lion coming after you for example, you had better run for your dear life my friend. That would be the right thing to do. Don't try to play the hero and try to confront the Lion. To do so would be unwise and your next appointment may well be in heaven.

Secondly, recognise that your beliefs influence a great deal of what you will eventually get to fear or not to fear. Therefore, challenge any beliefs that are consistently causing you to live in fear. Let them stand up to scrutiny. See whether other people react the same way to the things causing you to be afraid.

Thirdly, remember that fear stirs up your emotions, therefore, you can successfully deal with fear by choosing to rely on reason and 'cold facts' about the thing that is causing you to be afraid rather than relying on your emotions. This is a tough one to do, but with practice, over time, you will master how to do it.

I don't know who said it, but I find this acronym about FEAR very useful, it says; FEAR is **F**alse **E**vidence **A**ppearing **R**eal - the four letters that spell the word FEAR. **F** for False, **E** for Evidence, **A** for Appearing, and **R** for Real. And you know what? False evidence is another name for a lie, and only facts can sort it out. And that's why you need to search out the real facts of everything that is causing you to be afraid and properly evaluate it from the standpoint of those facts. Know your enemy, both literally and figuratively. Know what you are dealing with, get the facts, have the right perspective, evaluate any potential risks, and act out of an intelligently informed mind rather than a mind terrorised by fear. That is how to deal with fear; you face it head-on, wisely, confidently, and courageously.
Okay, so far, I have talked about taking full responsibility for the decisions and choices you make. I have also talked about ways to manage your desires and how to effectively take stock of your beliefs. Furthermore, I talked about how you can confidently deal with your fears.

Now, there is just one more thing I need us to consider in this discourse, and that is, your **Imagination**.

I don't know of anything that will help you to take charge of your life so effectively, and follow your

dreams, like Imagination does. In fact, nothing liberates or binds like Imagination, especially if you are ready and willing to have faith and act on what your imagination gives you.
Your Imagination is formless, boundless, and limitless. And whatever desires or fears you dwell upon with deep feeling and belief, your imagination takes them up, and moulds or forms them and returns them to you, embodied, in the screen of space - the physical world.
Your Imagination is a master craftsman and never fails to deliver, good or bad, according to what you have imagined with feeling and belief. When you deeply, and imaginatively dwell upon something and have your feelings about it wrapped up in faith, you are at that moment, creating that thing. Your imagination knows no bounds and knows no impossibilities.

Is not in the Bible where it is written that; "*All things are possible to him who believes*"? See Mark 9:23. And that is true of anyone in this world, regardless of race, religious affiliations, gender, or whatever.

You are a creator. And nothing is truly impossible to you in your creative state. If you did not know that, well, now you know. And you can use that knowledge to turn your life around for the better with creative imagination. You are powerful. Your Imagination is your creative force or power and the real essence of who you are.

Neville Goddard was a mystic and Bible expositor, and he had this to say about imagination; he said, "*I say imagination creates reality, and if this premise is true then imagination fulfils itself in what your life becomes. Although I have changed the words, what I am saying is not new. Scripture says it in this manner: "Whatsoever you desire, believe you have received it, and you will." This statement goes back two thousand years, yet even before that, Jeremiah tells of the same principle in his story of the potter and his clay. But until imagination becomes a part of your normal, natural currency of thought, you will not act consciously. Like breathing, this awareness must become so much a part of you that you will not turn to the left or the right to praise or blame anyone. When you know this presence, it will not matter if you started life behind the eight-ball, or in a palace; as a poor or a rich child; you will realize that life is always externalizing what you are imagining. Lacking the knowledge of this principle, you can reproduce your environment - be it pleasant or unpleasant - forever and ever, as you feed your imagination on what your senses dictate. But knowing this principle, you can ignore the present, and untethered by the so-called facts of life; you can imagine the present as you desire it to be and feed upon your desire, rather than its omission.*

Now, imagination cannot be observed as we see objects in space, for imagination is their reality. Faucett gives the name, "God" to the cause of the universe, saying: "God, the creator, is like pure imagining in ourselves. He works in the depths of our soul underlying all of our faculties, including perception, and streams into our surface mind least disguised in the form of productive fancy."

Listen to your thoughts, and you will hear God's words! A thought that is not felt produces nothing. But a thought producing motor elements reproduces itself! Catch God in a moment of a motor element such as anger, fear, or frustration, being congratulated or congratulating, and you will know what is going to happen in your world. Unless, of course, you arrest your thoughts and revise them. Most of us, however, are not aware of what we are doing, so we do not observe the creator. But we can catch him as he streams into our surface mind least disguised in the form of productive fancy. http://realneville.com/txt/imagination_fulfills_itself.htm

Now, as I conclude this chapter, let me ask you this; Are you following your dreams? And are you happy with the state of your life as it is now, or would you rather improve it and make it even better? Remember, any change you want to see in your life, must, of necessity start with you. You must change to realise the change you hope for. You have to rise in your consciousness and imagine yourself completely at one with the change you desire to see. In biblical language, it is called being transformed by the renewing of your mind.

The truth is, no one is responsible for your life but you. Not the government, not your mother-in-law, not your husband or your wife, not anyone of any race; black, white, or whatever colour, no, none of them. If they seem to be in control, it is because you have given them that power, but the responsibility for how your life eventually turns out, is still yours. And so, it makes a lot of sense, for you to unleash your personal power, and realise your personal freedom to run your life the way you want to.

Now, when you finally decide to take charge of your life, and start following your dreams, you shouldn't just jump in with both feet and put everyone on notice and tell them to back off because you are now in charge of your life, and that you will do things your way, from now on.

Ahh.., well, no. You don't do it like that. The idea is great, but the approach is somewhat comic and rude, and it might backfire on you. I am sure you want to be taken seriously and not be considered a joker, right? So, you have to do it wisely. Empowering yourself to take charge of your life and start following your dreams requires a new mindset and a plan.

So, work on yourself every day, renew your mind, and rather than short circuit your way to your dreams, grow into them. I sincerely hope that what you have read in this chapter has given you some ideas and actionable tips on how to go about getting started on your journey to positively changing something about the way you live your life and start following your dreams. The chapters ahead will reinforce what you have already got in this chapter.

Look, I don't know what your dreams are, or what it is you want to achieve in life. However, I want to challenge you to be courageous enough to be true to yourself and live your life authentically and start following your dreams. Don't live a life other people expect of you, but live one that you, yourself, determine upon, to live. People, including those closest to you, will expect all sorts of things from you. However, you will do well to learn how to manage those expectations as best as you can without compromising being true to yourself. And should you not fulfil some, or all of the expectation's others have of you, refuse to be weighed down by guilt, and get on with your life anyway, living it in the best way you can, standing strong and winning, no matter what you face in life. Be strong, be bold, be confident and courageous in your life, every day. Be authentically you and make no apologies for being so and keep developing yourself.

Transforming your life to live it the best way you can, starts with your mind. The scriptures put it this way, "*Be ye transformed by the renewing of your mind*" - Romans 12:2.

And you know what? Sometimes, the transformation takes time, therefore, you will need to be patient if things don't work out as fast or as smoothly as you want them to. The change will eventually happen if you stay on course and not give up. Stay plugged in, don't disconnect yourself from your aspirations, and your dreams. Feed your dreams through your imagination and be relentless in their pursuit.

And there you have it. If you are sick and tired of how things are in your life currently, and you want a change, then don't be afraid to go for it, even if that means starting all over again if you have to. This time you will not be starting from scratch, but rather from real valuable life experience. That is true authentic personal power at work here. Take charge of your life, command your destiny.

William Ernest Henley said this in Invictus: "*I am the master of my fate, I am the captain of my soul*"

Can you say the same about yourself?

> *Remember, any change you want to see in your life, must, of necessity start with you. You must change to realise the change you hope for. You have to rise in your consciousness and imagine yourself completely at one with the change you desire to see. In biblical language, it is called being transformed by the renewing of your mind.*

2

HOW TO STOP PROCRASTINATION AND BE MORE PRODUCTIVE

What you put off doing today, might cost you big tomorrow.

Have you ever found yourself wanting to do something but for some reason you decided otherwise and said to yourself, Mmmm..., I will do it tomorrow. Then tomorrow comes, and you say, I have been so busy today, I will definitely get it done tomorrow.

One day goes by, two days, three and counting, then one week, then two weeks, then one month, then three or six months, and before you know it, one year has gone by, and you have done nothing about what you wanted to do a year ago. And because you did not do that thing that you wanted to do six months or one year ago, you are probably now missing out on great opportunities to advance your career or business and follow your dreams.

Does that sound familiar?

Well, to be honest, I've been there before, and it is not at all a good place to be. But I also know that it is possible to stop this downward spiral of procrastination, and self-sabotage.

In this chapter, we will be considering how to get things done faster and successfully in your life and stop procrastination from ruining your chances and opportunities to advance in life.

Look, if you want to get things done faster in your life and accelerate your progress, you'll need to have nothing to do with procrastination, ever, in your life, and instead, learn to apply success principles in your life, principles like focus, and goal setting, for example.

Now, let me talk a little bit about goal setting. You have probably heard of the 'SMART' acronym when it comes to goal setting, haven't you? Well, I believe it is a good place to start from if you want to deal a death blow to the habit of procrastination and start getting things done in your life faster and successfully.

I think 'SMART' is a beautiful acronym to use in setting goals because it is a principle that gives you a clear understanding of how you should go about setting your goals and realising your dreams. It basically lays the foundation for getting things done faster.

'SMART' goal setting here means that your goals must be **S**pecific, **M**easurable, **A**ttainable, **R**elevant and **T**ime-bound or Time' sensitive.'

So, as we consider how to get things done faster, let us unlock the 'SMART' goal-setting formula. Shall we? Of course, why not.

So, **S** in **S**MART is for **Specific**

Now, if you want to get something done, you must specify exactly what it is you want done. A specific goal is well defined, something that can easily be articulated clearly and succinctly.

For Example, if your goal is to learn a new language,

A Non-specific way of putting that goal would sound something like this: I would like to learn a new language.

A Specific one on the other hand would be something like this: I am going to learn how to speak and write Hungarian fluently, for example.

Even better, you can state your goal in the affirmative, as if you have already achieved it. So, in this case, you would in *specific* terms say that; "*I speak and write Hungarian, fluently.*" How about that? That is called thinking with the end in mind, and it is a very powerful way of realising your goals if you understand the power of belief.

M in SMART is for **Measurable**

To be measurable in the context of getting things done means that your goal should have milestones to help you measure your progress, stay on track, and be accountable.

Staying with the goal of learning a new language, an Example of a non-measurable goal would be something like this: *I would like to learn a new language whenever I can.*

A Measurable goal in this case would be: *I am going to learn how to speak and write Hungarian starting tomorrow for 1 hour a day. You could also say more affirmatively (in the spirit of thinking with the end in mind) that; "I speak and write Hungarian for one hour every day."*

A in SMART is for **Attainable**

The things you want to achieve in life are only as attainable as you believe them to be so demonstrated by the appropriate actions you will take. There is a verse in the Bible that says that "*all things are possible to him who believes.*" Mark 9:23

Have absolute faith, and an unwavering confidence, that you will attain the object of your desire. That is, that it will be done, come what may.

Do not erroneously take the view as most people do, that your size or ability is the only thing that should determine whether you get things done. That could be a factor, but it is not the main one. The most important requirement here is your unwavering faith and conviction that, that which you desire to happen or to be done will be done. The ways and means of attainment will be revealed to you as you progress. Your faith is the pathway to that attainment.

The story of David and Goliath in the Bible is a very good illustration of this principle of faith - (see 1 Samuel 17:1 -end) David, had no doubt that the giant – Goliath would be brought down, and he did it. Read that story, it is quite fascinating.

Just believing only is not enough, you must act on what you believe for faith without works is dead.

Live, therefore, in an atmosphere, and consciousness of victory, and victory will be yours.

R in SMART is for **Relevant**

Of course. If you are to get something done at all, it must, of necessity be relevant, otherwise, it is a waste of time. But relevant to what? You may ask. Well, relevant to your mission, your dreams, or your purpose in life.

Irrelevant goals eventually leave you unfulfilled, often confused about your life's purpose and just existing as opposed to living. You might even end up getting paid much money for attaining your irrelevant goal, but what's the point of being so loaded with money but unfulfilled and unhappy? Money should not dictate relevance; Purpose should. Bear that in mind when deciding what goals to pursue.

T in SMART is for **Time-bound** or Time-sensitive.

This is all about having deadlines. When you want to get something done, put a deadline to it. Having no deadlines for what you want to achieve or get, is not that compelling and exhilarating.

My point here is this, don't have open-ended goals. Have deadline-driven goals. They are more likely to be attained than their open-ended counterparts.

Deadlines help you to focus your mind and attention and to unleash the power of your creative genius. That is what deadlines help you accomplish.

So, with all the above in mind, let me ask you this question; how big or grand should your goal be?

Well, I hope, as big or grand as you choose it to be! It is, after all, your life, make it as grand as you fancy. Only ensure that it is legitimate and authentic, and that you have not defrauded others along the way but have rather empowered them.

Shoot for the stars! The world is your Oyster.

That was all about 'SMART', goal setting, and what a brilliant concept it is for laying the foundation to getting things done faster.

Let us move on and consider an equally important aspect of getting things done and realising your dreams. I am talking about - **Preparation**.

You see, every human being I know wants to succeed; whether it is succeeding in their job, in their marriage, in their business or career, in their relationships, or in whatever it is that truly matters to them. Nobody likes to fail or goes out of their way to deliberately fail and enjoy doing so. No, it just doesn't happen.

Everyone wants to succeed. The question, however, is this; is everyone ready or prepared for success?

The Merriam Webster's online dictionary defines Preparation as the action or process of making something ready for use or of getting ready for some occasion, test, or duty.

An expectant mother, for example, will generally prepare for the arrival of her baby. A student will undergo gruelling days, months and even years of study to prepare for just a 3-hour exam that may well define the rest of his/her life.

The Olympic gold medallists take an enormous time to prepare for the final few minutes or even seconds of their act.

I am confident that your major accomplishments to date were well prepared for too; they did not just happen by accident, did they? Heck no! You did your very best to prepare for them, did you not?

And if you have missed any opportunities in your life, you will agree with me that it was because you were not adequately prepared for them in the first place.
So, it seems to me that being prepared is essential for success. You obviously don't know everything that is going to happen in your future, but you have a responsibility to prepare for those things that you know are likely to happen.

Yes, I know you cannot anticipate every possible development, but it helps to plan and practice for those you can anticipate. Just don't stumble into tomorrow or your future blindly. Prepare to enter into it wisely, and conscientiously by planning and preparing for it today.

Plan every step you will take as you edge ever so close to realising your goals. Visualise the beauty, the joy, the satisfaction of precisely living the way you desire.

You see, there is simply no substitute for PREPARATION. Preparation is a hallmark of faith. When you are prepared, there is that assurance you get within your heart, that, all is well.

Your dreams and destiny demand that you adequately prepare for them. However, if you become negligent and don't adequately prepare, it is possible that you will cause your own downfall. Therefore, take care to prepare, and prepare well.

And the key to being well prepared is **Planning and Practice**.

Plan then practice and practice some more. Practice both imaginatively and physically. Visualise the ideal situation repeatedly until you feel yourself really there and take relevant steps to realise that ideal.
It is worth remembering that if you don't have a plan, you have no protection against some of the unintended consequences of change and need I say, from time wasters and those who sabotage dreams. A plan does not only help you stay focused, but it also helps you,

albeit subtly, to avoid detours. And that is why you must have clear and definite plans for in your life.

A good plan is like a roadmap, it shows the destination and usually the best way to get there.

The truth is, you are 100% responsible for the way you live your life and the results you achieve in it as an adult. That responsibility is one you must never delegate or indeed take lightly.

It is better to have a plan for living your life and change it when necessary, than not have a one at all.

The late Dr Myles Monroe- an internationally known author, bible teacher, and leadership mentor once said; "*God's strategy for guaranteeing your future is planning. God Himself is a planner* – see Jeremiah 29:11.

God gave you a brain and the gift of imagination so that you can participate in creation through planning. And the highest expression of divine nature is planning".

Clarify what you want, then create a plan of action that delineates your path to realising your goal and avoid any irrelevant side-tracks.

Examine every project or venture you would like to get involved in, examine it in great detail. Study it thoroughly because it is crucial that you must know all the facts available to you to help you navigate your path with wisdom.

No acceptable reason in this day and age exists for not being well informed. Ignorance is inexcusable, and if you tolerate it, you will inevitably fail in life. Remember, being informed is a continuous and daily business and not a one-off thing.

Do your very best to limit surprises in your projects and avoid dismissing any potential problems as too minor or unlikely to happen. Don't do that. Instead, what you need to do is realistically assess the greatest downside liability for each potential problem that you face, price the cost of dealing with it in tomorrow's values and factor the time and resources it could cost you. And you must make sure that you have a financial cushion built up that will allow you to avoid being knocked off or squeezed out when problems and delays occur in the important projects of your life.

Now, plans require time for their execution. Don't they?

But here is the thing, there are only 24 hours in a day, and nobody lives forever. Therefore, to ensure that you make the most of each day you've got is of paramount importance, and a wise thing to do.

And that leads me to ask you this question; how are you using your daily 'time allowance' of twenty-four hours?

Arnold Bennett – one of the prolific English writers of the 19th century, said something so profound about time in his book - "**How to live on 24 hours**", and I would like to pass what he said, to you.

He said "*Philosophers have explained space. They have not explained time. It is the inexplicable raw material of everything. With it, all is possible; without it, nothing is.* ***The supply of time is truly a daily miracle****, an affair genuinely astonishing when one examines it.*

You wake up in the morning, and lo! Your purse is magically filled with twenty-four hours of the unmanufactured tissue of the universe of your life! It is yours. It is the most precious of possessions. A highly singular commodity showered upon you in a manner as singular as the commodity itself!

For remark! No one can take it from you. It is 'unstealable'. And no one receives either more or less than you receive.

Talk about an ideal democracy!

In the realm of time, there is no aristocracy of wealth and no aristocracy of intellect. Genius is never rewarded by even an extra hour a day. And there is no punishment. Waste your infinitely precious commodity as much as you will, and the supply will never be withheld from you. No mysterious power will say: 'This man is a fool, if not a knave. He does not deserve time; he shall be cut off the meter...'

No.

You have to live on these 24 hours of daily time. Out of it, you have to spin health, pleasure, money, content, respect, and the evolution of your immortal soul. Its right use, its most effective use, is a matter of the highest urgency and of the most thrilling actuality. All depends on that.

We shall never have any more time. We have, and we have always had, all the time there is. It is the realisation of this profound and neglected truth that has led me to the minute practical examination of daily time expenditure."

Wow! Did you hear that last bit – "*the minute practical examination of daily time expenditure.*"

How incredible! I like it.

You see, *"To everything, there is a season, and a time to every purpose under heaven"* - Ecclesiastes 3:1.

Do you know who said that?

King Solomon did. He is credited to be the wisest and richest king who ever lived, and history has proved him unequivocally right.

There is indeed a time and season to do everything 'under the sun'. Get the moment right, and it's blissful, get it wrong, and suffer the consequences.

Have you ever heard of the phrase; 'perfect timing', or 'timing is everything', or 'in the fullness of time'?
If so, do you have any idea how to know when it is the perfect time to do or say something?

Tell me, have you ever totally blown your chances or opportunities by saying or doing something at the wrong time?
Well, I have, and I have done it many times.

You know, I would have loved to delve deep into the subject of time management, but I realise that this is not a dossier on time management and besides, I think there is way lots of resources out there on that subject already.

What I would like to zero in, however, is the question of right timing, what I would like to call - The Moment.

Now, getting the moment right is very essential to anything you do.

And do you know what? You can deduce the success or failure of most things by considering their timing – the moment they were brought out into the world.

It doesn't really matter how great or wonderful a product or an idea or service is, if it's brought up at the wrong time, it's almost guaranteed to fail from the onset.

It is like timing calls the shots.

Here is what I have come to realise; perfect timing comes about when opportunity meets Preparation.

When an opportunity finds you prepared, the perfect timing is right there, staring you in the face. It is like hitting the bullseye.

We miss out a lot in life because we are impatiently rushing around and getting ourselves muddled up in all sorts of things and thereby getting tied up in gruelling routines, and never actually getting anywhere significant with our lives. It's like a hamster on its treadmill.

Like the master potter would do with clay; moulding beautiful things to behold, so too should we take time to let our imagination mould our desires while we get ready for their realisation.

Everything you need to do in this world requires time; there is no question about that. However, what is blatantly evident everywhere you go is that; the way people use time is not taken seriously.

I even dare say that time is one of the most misused or abused 'resources' in the world today, and it's no wonder that most people are stuck and broke in life despite all the abundance around them.

You see, time is one of your greatest allies in life, and learning how to master the use of your personal time, is, therefore, very, very, important.

If time is on your side, there is a lot you can accomplish. However, the story is different if you are 'working against time'. If you are running out of time; the pressure, the anxiety, the stress, is just too much, and the quality of your work can be severely affected.
So, I would like to propose that you take your time management, to a different level, to a high level of productivity.

I suggest you start living your life with a *functionally time-specific* mindset.

What do you mean by that Sterling, you may ask?

Let me give you an example to illustrate what I mean; say, the watch on your wrist or the clock on the wall reads 10:00 am; most people when asked what time it is would say that it is ten o'clock in the morning. And they are correct. However, as accurate as that may be, you should rather consider what your plan for the day is at 10:00 am, and then say what time it is based on the result you are hoping to achieve at that time. For example, if you were supposed to close some sales at 10:00 am, you would say; it is time to close some sales. Or to do the accounts, if that is what you had planned to do, etc.

Whatever it is you have planned to do at that time of the day, that is what the time is as far as you are concerned, and not the reading on the watch on your wrist or the clock on the wall. You do get my point, don't you?

As you may well know already, you get 24 hours every day, time to do whatever you wish to do, it is all up to you. Let me ask you this; wouldn't it be better to assign goal-oriented tasks to those 24 hours you receive daily, making sure that you account for each minute productively? Wouldn't that be great?

Please don't be like most people who seem not to know what to do with their time except spend it in wantonness, hopping from one thing to the other and spending their lives in a state of confusion, want and scarcity; yet there is abundance all around them.

To break free from limiting and defeating habits and patterns that have held and continue to hold you back in life, you should never, ever tolerate time-wasting in your life in any form or shape. Period.

To summarise what we have covered in this chapter, here is what you need to bear in mind and act upon:

- ✓ Be SMART about what you want to do,
- ✓ Plan and prepare for the things you want to see happen in your life. And finally,
- ✓ Don't waste time. Live by the principle of minute-by-minute practical examination of your daily time expenditure.

That is how you get things done and get them done faster and be on your way to realising your dreams.

And one more thing, here is something I often endeavour to do every morning upon waking up, it is immensely powerful in helping me get things done.

1. I decide or reaffirm exactly, what it is I want today, and I write it down, if I haven't yet.
2. then after that, I relax into a comfortable position, close my eyes, and try to see, feel, and experience what I want in my imagination.
3. And finally, once I have experienced it in my imagination, I then give thanks for having received that thing I wanted, and then I get on with the rest of the things and day.

It is a simple but very powerful exercise, and it works in helping me realise my dreams, and I am confident it will work for you too. How it works, I have no clue, but it works.

> *It is worth remembering that if you don't have a plan, you have no protection against some of the unintended consequences of change and need I say, from time wasters and those who sabotage dreams. A plan does not only help you stay focused, but it also helps you, albeit subtly, to avoid detours. And that is why you must have clear and definite plans for in your life*

3

HERE IS HOW TO RISE TO THE TOP IN YOUR CALLING

Never rest on your laurels. Ever heard of that?

I would like you to consider this for a moment: Year after year in the IAAF World Championships in Athletics, you see athletes breaking their own world records in mesmerising fashion. Many of these athletes show a performance that is a class apart from the previous year's competition just 12 months back, performed by these same athletes! What do you think made the difference one year later?

What about other sports competitions, like football, cricket, baseball, rugby, formular one, etc. you often find that the crowned world champions in these sports had tried and failed two, three or four times before they attained the coveted status of Champion(s).

And look at the rate of technological change and advancement in the world today; computer chips have become increasingly more powerful with every new upgrade released. The rate of progress technologically is mind-blowingly fast and unbelievably sophisticated. It is incredible.

Surely, the journey of athletes and sports stars from amateurs to champions, and the breakthroughs in technology and many other wonderful things we see happening in our world today just don't happen on their own accord, do they? Certainly not. There is something behind these remarkable and outstanding results.

In this chapter, we are going to explore the cause of such remarkable results, but more so in our own lives. We will explore how we can be champions in our own way of life, and see how we can do so consistently, with grace and dignity.

I would like to use snow to illustrate something here for you, something quite remarkable.

When it starts snowing, one snowflake falls over the other, one at a time, and as the temperature gets colder and colder, the snowflakes start sticking to one another. Over time, as the snow builds up and as the temperature decreases, the built-up snow starts turning into ice.

It is not uncommon to hear of schools not opening, or roads becoming impassable, and public transport severely disrupted, because of heavy snow. The snow has transformed itself into a weather phenomenon, slowly, and consistently, one snowflake at a time, one after the other. How remarkable!

The individual snowflakes in themselves could do nothing. However, given the right temperature and consistent snowing, the small snowflakes coming together over time, totally 'transform themselves' into a force to be reckoned with.

In a somewhat metaphorical sense, that is what happens to us also when we innovate and improve our way of life and the way we do things, doing so, little by little, step by step, consistently over time. We, also become formidable, and a force to reckon with in our own right.

Innovation, in my view, is the 'mother' of progress. Innovation is about effectiveness, it is about getting things done faster, cost effectively, smoothly, and beautifully. It is seen as the ability to discern a better way – **improving** on your last performance. It is, the greatest success factor of high achievers, it's their secret ingredient in the formular of success.

Here is my point, by consistently making little and small adjustments and improvements in certain key areas of your life, you can radically transform your life in a very, very wonderful, and profound way.

"The biggest room in the world is the room for improvement", said **Helmut Schmidt**

So, what areas of your life do you think could do with some improvements?

Well, to answer that question, let us consider the **Physical, Spiritual, Psychological, Intellectual,**

Emotional, Financial, Social, and Family aspects of our lives, and let's call them the Eight equities.

Now, I believe these are the eight areas of our lives, that when consistently improved, will make an enormous difference in the quality of life each of us lives, and to the contribution we make to this beautiful world we live in.

I am confident that when you do at least one thing every day that improves any of the above eight 'equities', the way you will experience life will never be the same, and your impact in the world around you will be very remarkable and powerful indeed, in this generation, and generations to come.

We will now look at improvements in the above eight 'equities' by broadly looking at Improvements in your TIME management, Your HEALTH and Your MIND which form a foundation for your core goals (Health & Energy, good career, excellent relationships, financial independence)

In each case, the decisive factor in the achievement of these goals that we all hold in common is the development of the specific habits that lead automatically and inevitably to the results that you want to achieve.

We'll begin by considering improvements in - **Your TIME usage**

I have already talked about time usage in my earlier discourse on "How to *Get Things Done Faster.*" However, it bears repeating, albeit at the risk of sounding monotonous. Time must not be squandered. It has been rightly said that; *'The rich and the poor have one thing in common, and that is, that they both have 24 hours every day'*. The difference, however, is on how they use these 24 hours.

Making money, building a family and relationship all require excellent time management skills.

From the many books written, and lectures given about time management, their central message is this: **You cannot save time, and time waits for nobody. So, use it wisely**. Full stop.

Time will continue to tick no matter what activity you do (whether it is valuable or not), time will not wait for you.

What you, therefore, decide to do with your daily allowance of 24 hours should be a matter of great importance to you. Shouldn't it?

Reassigning your time from activities of low value to activities of high value, would be a good use of your time. And what is of low value or high value is subjective, and that is up to decide for yourself. But just make sure that most, if not all of your time is dedicated to high value activities you decide upon.

You should structure your time usage in such a way that it continually supports you positively in the attainment of your goals and desires in life. Better still, plan today, how you are going to use tomorrows 24 hours – that is, plan your activities in advance other than just 'falling' into them, and one of the best ways of doing that is to have a frame of mind of not to just do things but rather one of performing them. There is a big difference between just doing something and performing it. Performance requires skill, attention, and planning. Animals do things, humans should perform things.

Let me explain...

When you are in a performance frame of mind, you will choose to carefully plan and programme yourself for the performance as opposed to when you are in a mental frame of 'just doing something'. The difference in outcome is huge, trust me, I know so. Be a committed and dedicated performer in your life.

Another great way to make excellent use of your time is to use it to get better at the most important things you do. If you are good at any sport, for example, use what most people call "free time" to practise getting better at your sports activity. If you are an artist, use that time to improve your artistic craft, etc.

Your goal ideally should be to upgrade your skills so that you achieve more and better results in a short space of time.

Remember, you will need time to do virtually everything. So, make it count, and make it count for something worthwhile. Be careful how you use your time.

With that, we now turn our attention to considering improvements in your health, and we'll be looking at both your physical and mental health.

Your Physical Health

It is important that you look after your physical health in a responsible way.

Why is that important?

Because there is a certain degree of peace you experience when you have a healthy body, when you don't have to be concerned about going to the doctor, when you can move, jump, swing, and dance as freely as you want to because your body is in good condition.

I don't know about you, but for me, having a healthy body has an impact on how I face and experience life. And having a healthy body does not come by accident, no it does not, you have to work at it, daily.

It pays to listen and act on the advice that doctors, and health professionals give about good physical health. For example, they comment that smoking is not good for any of us, and people should not do it. And you know what, I agree with them. I think that if God wanted us to smoke, He probably would have put a chimney on top of everybody's head, but as you may well know, He did not do that.

There is also the advice out there about having sufficient rest (sleep) for our bodies, which I think is excellent advice worth heeding. For you see, experts say that to not get enough sleep can lower your sex drive, weaken your immune system, cause thinking issues, and lead to weight gain. When you don't get enough sleep, you may also increase your risk of certain cancers, diabetes, and even car accidents.

Another good advice given by the experts for the welfare of our bodies is about eating in moderation and not in excess. Again, I think it is superb advice, and I couldn't say any less. The thing is, overeating can easily spiral out of control and lead to various negative health consequences. If you are given to too much appetite, seek help to curb it, otherwise, pretty soon you might have to face the inevitable consequences of overeating, and I tell you what, those consequences are neither desirable nor beneficial.

Fit for Life – a book by Harvey Diamond is a great book which reveals among other things,

- The secrets of timing and food combining that work with your natural body cycles.
- The three vital principles to bring permanent weight loss and high energy.
- A complete four-week meal plan, menus, delicious recipes, and essential shopping tips.

I heard about Fit for Life many years ago in my teens and I have used the principles in that book since then, and the results in my physical health are remarkable. I recommend that book to you – Fit for Life.

Other things the experts say will do your body wonders include things like; taking time to relax (doing recreational activities), smiling and laughter, and having a positive outlook to life, that is - not worrying. And guess what, that is really interesting because I read it somewhere, sometime ago, that nothing in life is worth the price of worry. So true. I agree, and guess what, millennia ago, Jesus Christ paused a very profound question to his listeners, and I think it is still a very relevant question today, and it is this: "*Can anyone of you by worrying add a single hour to your life*" Matthew 6:27. Think about that next time you are tempted to worry about anything. Will you, by worrying, be able to add a single hour to your life? I am sure you know the answer perfectly well, don't you?

How about **Earthing** or **Grounding,** have you heard of it? It is said to be very good for the human body.

"*Years of extensive research has shown that connecting to the Earth's natural energy, by walking barefoot on grass, sand, dirt or rock can diminish chronic pain, fatigue and other ailments that plague so many people today. This connection is referred to as Earthing or Grounding.*

To put it briefly, when your bare feet or skin comes in contact with the earth, free electrons are taken up into the body. These electrons could be referred to as nature's biggest antioxidants and help neutralise damaging excess free radicals that can lead to inflammation and disease in the body. The Earth is a conductor or free electrons and so are all living things on the planet, including us.
The Earth is a conductor or free electrons and so are all living things on the planet, including us. The body is composed of mostly of water and minerals which in combination are excellent conductors of electrons from the Earth providing

there is direct skin contact or some other conductive channel for them to flow through.

The Earth's energy upgrades one's physiology by allowing the body to cope and repair thereby promoting wellbeing, vitality, and better sleep. It also harmonizes and stabilizes the body's basic biological rhythms, knocks down (and even knocks out) chronic inflammation and reduces and eliminates associated pain, making it the most natural and powerful anti-inflammatory and anti-aging remedy around! No matter what your age, gender, race or health status you will benefit from a daily dose of Earthing!" https://www.barefoothealing.com.au/v/what-is-earthing/22

Anyway, the bottom line is this, please do yourself a favour and take very good care of your body.

You need your physical body to do physical stuff in this world of form and substance. The day you lose your physical body, that is the day you cease to exist in this world physically.

So, to keep your body healthy and strong, is, therefore, something you should take seriously indeed.

Next, we will now move on and consider **Your Mental Health.**

Your mental health, in my view, has a lot to do with your faith and belief system.

Now, there are a lot of challenging and demanding circumstances or conditions that can happen in your life, sometimes at the most unexpected times and ways. Many of these circumstances may push your patience and your beliefs to their limits, and you might experience a lot of frustration, anger, resentment or even depression.

You see, the drama of life is a psychological one, in which all conditions, circumstances and events of your life are interpreted and acted upon based on your beliefs.

Transforming your mental health starts with an examination of your beliefs and an honest openness to admit that not all that you believe is necessarily true or appropriate.

I will expound more on beliefs in the next section – your Mind, but for now, here are five things I often do to help keep my mental health in top condition, and I commend these five things to you too.
They are:

1. Be an avid reader, and whenever possible, read out loud to yourself or somebody for at least a minimum of 25 minutes each time for at least three days in week.
2. Fully accept yourself. Be authentically true to yourself, consistently. Don't pretend to be someone else in order to get validation or acceptance.
3. Take time to be quiet. Practice silence and stillness. Meditate for at least 20 to 30 minutes a day if you can.

4. Be thankful—express gratitude for big and small things alike in your life.
5. Choose to forgive others and do it with no preconditions. Don't hold grudges.

However, if you are currently in bad shape and in need of some urgent mental health help, please go and see a therapist or a professional as soon as you can.

Now, so far, we have looked at how to improve your **Time management**, and how important that is for your finances, family, and relationships. We also looked at how to improve your **health (physical and mental)**, and why that is important too.

Let's now move on and look at...

YOUR MIND

Now, this is what I call the epicentre of what your existence as a human being is. What happens here, affects how you use your time and how you value your health, and ultimately, how you achieve your goals, and champion the course of your life.

Most unprecedented changes in people's lives happen by improvements in their minds first. No wonder Apostle Paul said: *"...but be ye transformed by the renewing of your mind..."* Romans 12:2. Transformation in your life is brought about by the renewing of your mind first.

In the eight equities I stated earlier on (Physical, Spiritual, Psychological, Intellectual, Emotional, Financial, Social and Family), half of them fall under -

your mind and these are: psychological, intellectual, emotional, and spiritual, and they are very powerful in that they help form your core beliefs and attitudes in life.

Ask yourself this question; do I currently hold empowering or self-limiting beliefs?

You see, one of the most important things you can do to enhance the way you experience life is to challenge your self-limiting beliefs.

Why do I say so?

Because your beliefs eventually determine your habits, and your habits 'make or break you'. You can't help being habitual in life, it is wired into your DNA, and you will always have habits, and there is nothing you can do about that. What you can do, however, is help yourself by developing good habits, ones that will be empowering and not debilitating, and that starts with the kind of beliefs you decide to hold dear.

Undoubtedly, changing your beliefs is one of the most challenging things you will ever do, but none the less, the most important thing you will have to do if those beliefs are limiting you.

I have some good news for you though, given the fact that all beliefs are learned, you can also unlearn any beliefs, especially if they are limiting or destructive.

Your beliefs form your life support structures, and that is why you should regularly take stock of them and see whether they are empowering you in life or causing you to live a frustrating and mediocre life. Be brutally honest with yourself in this exercise. Maybe you might have to seek the help of a professional in this exercise.

Here is the thing, your beliefs define what is possible for you. They act as a lens and yardstick through which you view, measure, and relate to the world around you. They decide how you should behave, what kind of person would make a good partner for you, and what really matters in the world for you. They determine what is right or wrong, and what is good, or bad, for you. Your beliefs are powerful, don't underestimate them.

And Power without accountability is very dangerous, and that is why I recommend that you regularly bring your beliefs to account by questioning or reviewing them. The good news is that you are always the de facto boss in your own life, and that means that you can change your beliefs at any time or point in your life if you want to. You don't have to be held hostage by limiting beliefs if you don't want to. You are the boss.

So, reviewing your beliefs is vital if you wish to expand your field of possibilities. Those who don't review their beliefs, let those beliefs run the show, and mostly from the shadows. Don't let that happen to you.

My suggestion is that you write down the beliefs you currently hold and start reviewing them. Remember, reviewing or questioning your beliefs does not mean changing them, no, at least that is not the objective here. The objective is to empower yourself by embracing empowering beliefs and discarding limiting ones. When you do that, a door to a new world will open before you each time a limiting belief you've held for so long is debunked.

Ask yourself the following questions about each belief you have written down:

1. When did I first start believing .... (the belief)?
2. Who taught me, or where did I learn it from?
3. Did I ever question this teaching or seek to educate myself on the issue from various multiple sources?
4. What would happen if I changed my mind on this issue? Or, what if I believed its opposite? (*One way to find out is to do the 'what if' with an open mind and see what happens*).
5. Have I ever discussed this issue with someone who disagrees or sees it differently?

Pause a bit here, and seriously consider the above five statements before moving on.

Now, whenever you feel disempowered in life, check to see what sort of beliefs you hold about whatever is causing you to feel disempowered. Chances are, you hold self-limiting beliefs about that thing. And if so, gather the courage to embrace more empowering beliefs, and liberate yourself.

Another thing you can do about disempowering beliefs is to talk to someone you trust about what you feel is disempowering you and be open minded to any suggestions and help they might offer you. But don't blindly act on their suggestions and advice, though you trust them. Think about your situation and take their advice and suggestions in context. Have your own mind, be independent in thought. Nothing wrong with that.

Keep your mind renewed daily.

Keeping your mind always renewed is one of the best ways to take responsibility for your life and certainly a wise way of taking advantage of the changing circumstances of life as time goes by.

Discipline yourself to shape your personality and character in almost any way you desire by renewing your mind.

The thing is, there is virtually nothing you cannot accomplish if you put your mind to it. History is full of evidence showing how what seemed impossible in one generation was proved wrong in another generation years later.

Consistent improvement in the little things over time makes a huge difference. You should always strive to improve on your last performance. Commit to living a life of continuous IMPROVEMENT. Do it by practice and repetition and being imaginative. On many occasions, you will have to persevere and persist. But hang in there, the payoff is worth it. Keep taking the baby steps, they all add up eventually.

Achieving your breakthrough and transformation in life will require you to be determined, resilient and to have a relentless drive to improve on your last performance.

In closing, here is what I recommend you keep in mind; if a thought crosses your mind of some action you can take to IMPROVE the quality of your life, - evaluate it, and if sound, then just do it! Be an action-oriented individual.

Obviously, along the way, you are bound to make mistakes. However, you don't know where the edge lies until you've been over it. Take one step at a time.

I believe by now you will agree with me that there is no one responsible for your success and breakthroughs in life but yourself. So, don't let yourself down, have faith and confidence in yourself, for that's how you have faith and confidence in God. Imagine great things for yourself and the world around you, and then have the courage to do what the infinite intelligence, the inner voice within you says as it guides you.

Like I said before, you are the one who is responsible for how things turn out to be in your life, and that includes the state of your health, your wealth, and your relationships. If you don't like the state of any of them, it is 100% within your power to do something about it and IMPROVE it or change it. You run the show in your life, don't forget that.

Peace and Love to you. Let's move on and consider how to stay focused in life, next.

Most unprecedented changes in people's lives happen by improvements in their minds first. No wonder Apostle Paul said: "...but be ye transformed by the renewing of your mind..." Romans 12:2. Transformation in your life is brought about by the renewing of your mind first.

4

HOW TO STAY FOCUSED IN YOUR LIFE

You must discipline yourself to stay on course and never entertain distractions if you want to achieve noteworthy success.

Not everything vying for your attention will lead you to success. In fact, some of them will cause you lots of trouble if you give them your attention.

Choose what matters most to you and give it all the time it demands and avoid overloading yourself with lots of things to do.

In short, you must discipline yourself to prioritise and stay focused if you are to achieve noteworthy success.

Achievers often work with a sense of priority, and they are resolute and determined. They are focused.

I have achieved quite a bit in my life so far, and I can confidently say that being focused helped a lot. To be focused is all about:

- ✓ Being attentive, aware, and zeroed in on the things that matter.
- ✓ It is about avoiding things and circumstances that will distract you from your main goal.
- ✓ It is about belief and faith.
- ✓ And it is also about planning, and taking action, and finally,
- ✓ It is also about being accountable.

Here is also something you need to bear in mind about being focused, it is this, when you decide to focus on something that is very important to you right now in this season of your life, inevitably, you will get out of balance in relation to all other things vying for your attention.

When that happens, don't worry so much about that and don't lose heart. Keep the main thing the main thing and counterbalance all others. Only make sure that you maintain sufficient control over those other things for them not to get completely out of control.

Whatever your topmost goal is currently, whether it's to be a successful entrepreneur, or getting married, or getting more money, I don't know what it is, but whatever it is, if you must achieve it, then you must focus your attention on it. For where attention goes, the power to achieve also follows.

But the power to achieve is most effective when you believe that you will realise the outcome of what you are focussed on. Faith is essential. Having faith will greatly magnify the power of your focus and your resolve to attain your objectives. You must, of necessity, believe that you already have what you desire. You must see the outcome or the end in your mind's eye, so to say.

Let your imagination lead the way. See what you want, feel it, and believe it is yours now.

That said, as important as being focused is, success in this life is not 100% just a mind thing; it is also an action thing. You need to be action oriented.

And there are two types of actions you should be familiar with,

1. common-sense actions, and
2. inspired actions.

A common-sense action is an action based on common sense, and inspired actions are based on inspiration or intuition.

Say, for example, you want to start a new business, selecting your company name, registering it with the government agency, getting all the paperwork done, etc., would be common-sense actions.

Inspired actions, on the other hand, would be the actions you would take based on your imagined outcomes, including but not limited to following through with the ideas and suggestions that pop up in your mind in relation to your dreams and aspirations, as well as engaging in positive affirmations and confessions.

Inspired actions would also include things like being self-assured, exuding confidence and acting as if you already possess it or have attained it – whatever the "it" is.

In a way, you basically claim to be or to have that thing you desire to be or have, and you do it without any shadow of a doubt that it is so. It is about putting your faith to work.

Sometimes taking an inspired action may seem so trivial, daunting, or even ridiculous. However, please do not neglect to take it. It is the inspired actions that will count for many significant breakthroughs in your life.

A focused life is quite something powerful, really powerful. The men and women who have made the greatest difference in human history were very focused individuals. Apostle Paul, for example, almost single-handedly spread Christianity throughout the Roman Empire back then. Imagine that! What an accomplishment. And guess what, that was made possible because of his focussed life. Here is what he said as recorded in Philippians 3:13, NLT, he said: "*...I focus on this one thing: forgetting the past and looking forward to what lies ahead*". We have billions of Christians all over the world today, and there is no doubt as to Pauls hand in this remarkable achievement. Laser focused and following the promptings and guidance of the Holy spirit. What a life.

In concluding this short but important chapter on how to stay focused in life, I would like to reiterate that, in life, it is your responsibility to choose what to focus your attention on. And I hope you will focus it on the things that matter most to you, great things that you want to see manifest in your life, otherwise, if you don't, well, let's just say, it will miss out on great things in life.

I hope you will choose to focus your attention on what you want and not on what you don't want, and always affirm your desires with conviction and faith, and then take the necessary action to realise them.

Let's move on and talk about Money and Wealth.

> *Here is also something you need to bear in mind about being focused, it is this, when you decide to focus on something that is very important to you right now in this season of your life, inevitably, you will get out of balance in relation to all other things vying for your attention.*

5

MONEY AND WEALTH

What they never told you about money, but you are now going to know.

George S Clason in his financial classic – The Richest Man in Babylon, said something so profound, something that will liberate you financially if you put it into practice. He said: "***A part of all you earn is yours to keep***".

What George said there is very powerful. It is a very simple but powerful money principle, one that if implemented, will transform your finances. However, it is one of those life principles that is easy to talk about, but one that requires enormous discipline to implement. And at the heart of this principle is the simple practice of **paying yourself first**.

In this chapter, I am going to show you why you might not have enough money in your life, and what you can do about it. And I will also show you that there is more to money than what you are accustomed to, or what you have been taught so far. So, get ready.

Your Journey to Financial Freedom

Now, you might be wondering, what does he mean by pay yourself first? How does that work? Isn't all the money I earn mine?

Well, to a certain extent, the answer is yes, because you earned that money, true, but on the other hand, the answer is no, because as soon as you get paid, you then start paying lots of other people (The landlord, the bank for the mortgage, the grocer, the creditor, the shoemaker, the clothmaker, the car dealer, etc.) and before you know it, all the money is gone, and somehow, nothing is left over for you, you 'forgot' to pay yourself! All the money has gone out to pay other people. See, what you thought was yours, is not yours anymore.

For some of you reading this right now, you've probably worked hard for a very, very long time in your life, many, many years perhaps, but if I were to ask you what you have to show for all those years of hard work, you might struggle to do so. In fact, you might even be worried now about not having enough money for retirement, or for supporting the kind of lifestyle you desire to have later in life. For all those years you've worked, you have been paying everybody else but yourself, and now at the end of it all, zero, nothing left for you! Something is not right with this state of affairs. It shouldn't be so.

You see, in the final analysis, it is not what you receive from your employer or client that matters or counts, but what you keep.

Here is the thing, I believe that the reason most people struggle to pay themselves, and I have been there before myself, is because of what each of us calls our necessary expenses, which somehow always seem to grow to equal our incomes unless we protest to the contrary.

What many of us do is confuse what our necessary expenses are, from our desires. Often, we think that because I have earned a little more this time, I may gratify all these desires I have.

The truth, however, is that each of us, together with our good families are burdened with more desires than whatever income we may receive at any time, can gratify. It is folly to believe that you can gratify every desire you have. Your desires are a multitude and those that you may gratify are but a few. And the more money you earn, the more your desires seem to grow. They are like a bottomless pit, goodness me!

And so, the best way to guard yourself against being broke not long after you have received your income, is to **remember to pay yourself some reasonable percentage of your earnings, and budget for your necessary expenses and charitable giving, making sure that you discipline yourself to live within your means, then invest (***but seek advice first***) that portion you pay yourself, and start building a financial estate.** You could say in one sentence that, *that is the one commandment about managing your money properly.*

I know it is not an easy thing to do despite its simplicity, but you must do it if you want to succeed financially.

To ensure that you pay yourself first and that you don't spend more than you earn, strict and consistent budgeting is essential. And you must make sure that you stick to the budget. Don't budget, and then ignore your budget, that would defeat the whole purpose of prudent money management. Make sure that you understand and know where each penny you let go is going to, and for what purpose, otherwise hold on to every penny.

Write out a list of things you desire to do with the income you receive, then select those things that are necessary and others that are possible through the expenditure of no more than 90% of your income at most. After that, gather the courage to cross out the rest of the things in the list and consider them but part of that vast sea of desires that must go unsatisfied for now and regret them not.

The purpose of a budget is to help you to be prudent in the way you use your income. You should use it to help you sort out your necessities and in as far as attainable, your other desires. Use it to defend your financial estate from being eroded by your casual wishes & desires.

Your budget is like a searchlight that shows the dangerous spots to avoid in your journey to financial freedom and abundance, and if your finances have to improve, budgeting must be at the forefront as a tool for prudent stewardship of your money.

I believe that one of the greatest financial sink holes that we are all prone to fall into from time to time, is our impulsive nature. This nature is in all of us but at varying degrees. The more pronounced it is in a person, the worse that person's financial situation is.

"*Impulsivity, or an impulsive behavior, is broadly defined as actions without foresight that are poorly conceived, prematurely expressed, unnecessarily risky, and inappropriate to the situation. impulsive behaviors can also lead to financial and legal harm if left unchecked.*" https://www.verywellmind.com/impulsive-behavior-and-bpd-425483

Each of us will do well to have our impulsive behaviour or nature in check. Curb it, so to say, and don't let your impulses have the best of you.

Now, paying yourself first from your earnings or income is a prudent thing to do, and you should save up those amounts you pay yourself, and use them to buy or acquire assets and investments that will then generate more and more income for you.

Furthermore, instead of using up the income your investments generate, why not reinvest most of it? If you did that, that is; buy assets and investments with what you pay yourself and reinvest the income those assets or investments generate, to buy more assets and investments. It will just be a matter of time before you become a money titan because of one of the wonders of the world called **Compound interest**.

What I have suggested above is not a get rich quick scheme and as such, you will need to be patient and disciplined before the big bucks start rolling in, and the earlier you begin doing this in your life, the better. The momentum will build over time, that's for sure. The principle or power of compounding or compound interest will work in your favour. If you are reading or listening to this and you are in your early twenties, this is a good time to get started. However, if you are a bit older, that shouldn't stop you from getting started either. It is never too late to start. And I would also urge you to encourage your children, nieces, and nephews to start doing what I am suggesting here as soon as they start earning money in their lives.

Albert Einstein famously said that compound interest is the most powerful force in the universe. He said, "*Compound interest is the 8th wonder of the world. He who understands it, earns it; he who doesn't, pays it.*" Well, what can I say, I certainly won't argue with such a smart guy.

Now, what I have been saying so far in this chapter has been more of what is commonly understood about money, the sort of obvious but less implemented stuff. And I commend it to you and recommend that you take it seriously.

However, there is more, and I would like to talk to you more about the less obvious stuff that is nonetheless the most important and can really have an enormous impact on your financial wellbeing and success. It is what I call the foundation of financial abundance.

Let's begin by first understanding what money is, that is, understanding what its true nature is.

Henry George was an American political economist and journalist, and he once remarked that: "***Money*** *is not* *wealth although it may be exchanged for wealth. Wealth is tangible,* ***money****is intangible. Whilst the* ***true nature of money****is abstract, over the ages it has taken many tangible forms e.g., shells, metals, coin, paper notes and tokens of debt etc. It is in essence, however, distinct from any and all the forms it may take."* The Nature of Money – Land&Liberty https://www.landandliberty.net/henry-george%E2%80%99s-view-on-money/

I would like to zero in on what Henry George said about money being *intangible, and its true nature being abstract.* I believe there is a lot of truth in what he said. I fundamentally believe that *money is your capacity to imagine and create something for the benefit of others, and the confidence others place on you for what you do for them.* That's Money.

Here is the thing, your imagination is limitless, and can get you anything you want if you know how to use it. It will open the doors to whatever you want, so to say, and give you means and ways in the natural world for appropriating what you have believably imagined.

Now, most of us know money as notes and coins in the different denominations each country has, however, the real essence of money is that **Money is spiritual, and it resides in the realm of Faith and Confidence, and in the proper use of imagination.**

The notes and coins (currency) you see around in different countries, each with their own denomination is just a way of giving tangible form to faith and confidence, instead of having them as abstract things.

Let me explain.

You see, whenever you have received money (notes and coins), it invariably was because the person who gave it to you had faith and confidence in what you did for them or in what you are going to do for them. And the way they could show that confidence was with the notes and coins – the observable currency in use.

And likewise, whenever you have given out cash to somebody for the product or service they offered or had to offer you, you were merely expressing your confidence in them for what they did for you. You may well have given them cows, or goats, or gold, or digital currency, or whatever the currency of the day would otherwise have been. You get what I mean?

Even in the stock market or the currency market, there too, confidence is very critical, and this confidence is called Market confidence. Individuals and companies can lose or gain vast sums of "money" just based on the movement of confidence level of the Market (the Market being the mass mind composed of those people involved in the day-to-day stock or currency market trading)

Faith and confidence are critical aspects of money without which money, the notes, and coins, will be hard to come by, and with it (Faith and confidence), there is no limit on how much money you can have. As for long as you continue using your capacity to imagine, and confidently use that imagination of yours in meaningful and beneficial service to others, there is literally no limit to how much money you can have.

So, don't chase after the notes and coins, it is like chasing after the wind, you'll never catch it. Focus rather on using your imagination to add value in the marketplace of human interactions, and the notes and coins will consequently follow you, because people will have faith and confidence in what you do for them, and as such they will show it physically by the notes and coins, they'll give you.

When you stop living imaginatively, and people start losing faith and confidence in what you do to meet their needs, you will know it, the notes and coins will stop coming your way.

So, if you want to get money - the notes and coins, don't just sit there, you need to engage your imagination and have faith in your ability to contribute to the wellbeing of humanity and their interconnectedness. Let your imagination go to work to show you how to add value in the marketplace of human interactions. Then have the courage to put into action, the insights you receive from what your imagination gives you.

Let me give you five things you can do to clear the path for effortless and abundant money flow in your life.

i. Ask yourself this question; What have I got?

And don't even start thinking that you have nothing. As a matter of fact, you actually have a lot but just don't know that you do. Let me show you; just think about what you have in terms of say, your attributes, material things, your experiences, your talents, skills (hard and soft skills), Ideas, ideas which you can turn into products or services, your capacity to imagine, etc. You have a lot within you, it is unbelievable, and you are so full of potential. Pause, and take stock of what you have.

Alternatively, try to find out what challenges or problems people are facing in the marketplace of human interaction, and see what talents, experience, skills, and ideas you may have that can help alleviate or solve those problems or challenges.

ii. Once you've noted what you have, or understood what the marketplace needs, ask yourself how you can use those things you have to serve others and get paid for doing so.

You see, there are people out there who are willing and ready to pay for what you have. Go through all the things you have listed in step i above and choose the best one(s) to monetise through service to others. The secret to financial abundance is in giving; sharing what you have with as many people as possible. Life is boring and not good if you live it alone. Even God said that it is not good for man to be alone. So, you see, other people are an essential part of a good life.

iii. After step i and ii above, step three is to find out who exactly will benefit most from what you have to share or give.

This is what is popularly known in business as market research, finding your ideal or right fit client.

iv. Once you get to know who the best fit for what you have is, let them know that you have something that will enormously benefit them, and show them how they can get it.

This, in business, is what is known as marketing and sales. And if properly done, you'll start seeing an influx of people willing and ready to pay for what you have.

v. Once you start receiving these people, serve them excellently, exceedingly well, with grace dignity, and Love while they are with you.

This, in business, is called Customer service and care.

If you do the above five things **consistently** well, money (the notes and coins) will start looking for you, and it will find you, and not you, looking for, or chasing after it.

One thing that will stop you right on your tracks in following the above five steps is having a mindset of lack and deficiency. I, therefore, want to caution you in the strongest terms possible, to desist from having or entertaining that kind of mindset. I know it is a very common mindset, but you don't want to be one of those with it, especially if you want financial freedom. Having that sort of mindset is financially very debilitating.

The truth is, there is a lot of abundance in the universe, not lack. And this abundance is unlocked by your imagination powered by faith in confident service to others.

The mindset of lack and deficiency is a dangerous one, and you should not venture anywhere near it. This mindset is characterised by Doubt and Greed.

Now, let me ask you this; what good thing can come out of doubt and greed? Absolutely nothing good, only trouble. Doubts and greed lead people to be overprotective, stingy, and cantankerous, and as a result, they then start devising all sorts of shenanigans to get money.

Here is the thing, *just care deeply about what you do in serving others in the marketplace of human interactions and never entertain the idea of lack, or the idea of being self-centred, and the money will come your way.* There is an abundant supply in the universe, and all you have to do is make a demand. And the demand is most effectively made, like I have said before, through faith using your imagination in selfless service to others.

The abundance in the universe is inexhaustible, and it is available to all of us. But it is your responsibility to go and get what you want.

Now, notwithstanding the fact that there is an infinite abundance in the universe, and all are welcome to partake of it, why does poverty continue to prevail in the world?

I think that is a reasonable question to ask because the evidence is there in every nation of the world for all to see. In every nation, there are poor or very poor people. They struggle to make ends meet, even just meeting their basic needs. And yet, in the same nations, there are rich and very rich people. They have lots and lots of money - the notes and coins, stashed away in some bank, and they are living really big – you can tell it.

Why the disparity?

My experience and understanding tell me that, those who are rich and wealthy, whether in the past, present or in the future are the people who understand human needs and are constantly anticipating challenges or difficulties because of human desires and mistakes. They then engage their imagination to find solutions to those needs and challenges and then position themselves as the people who have the solutions to those challenges ready to be deployed, in service to their fellow human beings. And with that, they start commanding the confidence of others through the solutions they provide.

Pretty soon, the increased confidence they command is evidenced by the enormous amounts of notes and coins they amass and lo and behold, they become rich, very rich, and extremely rich.

Some of those who don't have much money – in my view, have not yet figured out the best ways to put their imagination to work to anticipate and solve human challenges, problems, and dilemmas well, but one day, they might have a breakthrough if they continue to diligently utilise their capacity to imagine.

Others have just resigned to the idea that poverty is a virtue and being rich is somehow evil. For such people, a radical shift in their beliefs about wealth, money and poverty is needed, otherwise they will stay poor for a very, very long time.

Erroneous beliefs about money, and the lack of understanding of the fundamentals of money and wealth creation has got some people, of every race and colour, all over the world too stooped in all sorts of superstitions and shenanigans in an attempt to either become rich or avoid poverty or maintain piety. Ever heard of the get rich quick schemes? Or money is evil? Well, don't fall for them, they are not true, and they will keep you grounded on poverty lane for decades.

I believe there is no secret to being wealthy. But if there is one, it is this - *just solve people's problems well and to their satisfaction, and be disciplined financially, and you will be on your way there*. And if you have not yet figured out how to solve people's problems or meet their needs, partner with someone who has, and support them. Buying stocks in companies that are serving human needs exceedingly well, for example, is one way of doing so. The result is the same, you too will be rewarded. However, remember to be disciplined and self-controlled, otherwise, you will find that whatever reward you get for solving other people's problems will just flow out from you to solve your many unending challenges or problems, that are being fostered by your uncontrolled desires and financial mistakes. And hence you will stay on ground zero and never rise in the ranks of having a surplus that will qualify you as either rich, very rich or extremely rich.

Just remember that long lasting WEALTH is hidden in lovingly solving other people's problems and in being disciplined and self-controlled in your life. That is where true wealth lies. Becoming wealthy is not a secret, and it has never been.

Anyone can become wealthy if they want to. There are way too many desires, challenges, and mistakes being made in the world today than they ever have been. And those mistakes, challenges, and desires present great opportunities for service to those with a servant's heart.

Does it matter that you are a bit advanced in years, if you are, and therefore, it might be too late for you?

O hell no! But it depends on your mindset.

Let's look back, and see what history has to tell us about it.

Here are 10 historical figures who got rich after 50:

1. **Harland Sanders:** *"Colonel" Sanders, the Founder of KFC, became a millionaire at 74.*
2. **Charles Darwin:** *Became wealthy after he published "The Origin of Species" at 50.*
3. **Taikichiro Mori***:* *Japanese economics professor quit his job at 55 to become a real estate tycoon.*
4. **Ray Kroc:** *Convinced the McDonald's brothers to franchise the fast-food restaurant at 52.*
5. **Grandma Moses:** *Had her art featured at the Museum of Modern Art at the age of 78.*
6. **Wally Amos:** *Sold the "Famous Amos" cookie brand at age 49.*
7. **Pablo Picasso:** *The famous artist didn't become a major success until his later years.*

8. **Laura Ingalls Wilder:** *Published her first book in the famous "Little House" series at 65.*
9. **Henry Ford:** *Introduced the first mass-production moving assembly line for cars at 50.*
10. **Judge Judy:** *Her infamous TV show first aired when Judy was 54 years old.*

And many, many, more other people.

Conversely, there are many, many, young people who are very well-off financially because they have found a way to serve human needs or solve problems in a remarkable way. And so can you.

There are countless opportunities more than ever in our generation for you to make a difference in people's lives and then be handsomely rewarded for doing so. And who knows, pretty soon we might see or hear about you in the headlines of the rich list. But even if you don't make it to the headlines, you have a real chance of living the life you desire, but it must of necessity, come by helping a lot of other people to live theirs, and doing so with Love and integrity.

There are over seven billion people in the world today, and all of them will always have desires, challenges, and will always make mistakes - they cannot help doing so. Desires will always demand fulfilment and mistakes will always need to be sorted out one way or the other. And if you can find a way to consistently meet your fellow human beings' desires and help solve their problems or difficulties to their satisfaction, you will surely be handsomely rewarded, and just as surely as the sun will rise tomorrow, Money will find its way to you, beyond your wildest dreams.

The hardest thing, however, about becoming wealthy, lies in the difficulty to rid yourself of selfishness, and bad habits. That is where the hard battle is.

And so, like everything else, true wealth also comes at a price, and I think the price is fair – *selfless and wholehearted devotion to serve one another in love; regardless of race, gender, ideology, or religion, and the discipline to hold yourself accountable*. That's the price, and pay it you must, if you want to succeed financially and be wealthy. It is a fair price.

Now, whether you are wealthy or are on your way there, the principles concerning the acquisition and accumulation of money and wealth stay the same, and they are:

1. *You need a source of income to begin with. Income is a very important constituent of the building blocks for wealth, and Income comes by getting paid for the value you produce in the marketplace of human interaction. You can offer value through paid employment or through your own business.*
2. *Pay yourself not less than 10% from your take home pay. Remember, part of what you earn is yours to keep. No if's or but's, make it a rule.*
3. *Invest the money you pay yourself by buying income generating asset(s) and investment(s).*
4. *Reinvest the income or interest you receive from your assets and investments to create momentum in the building of your financial estate and take advantage of compound interest.*
5. *Budget your expenses making sure that you never overspend. Live within your means.*

6. *Increase your ability to earn, that is, improve your skills and business offering, have more interest in your work, concentrate more on your tasks and stay resolute and persistent. Don't easily give up.*
7. *Protect yourself and your financial estate through insurance (speak to a financial advisor for advice and guidance in this area)*
8. *Your mind is your greatest money making 'machine' and you should secure it and diligently guard and protect it. Put your imagination to work, don't restrain it. Your imagination knows the deeper secrets of money and wealth. Be open-minded*
9. *Your financial life support structures are your beliefs, especially your beliefs about money. Hold or have empowering beliefs about money, and life, and ditch the ones that are self-limiting and superstitious.*
10. *Give. Give to Charity. There is something unique about giving that makes you accumulate more money. I don't know what it is, but giving cheerfully to help others in need, in business or otherwise, enhances your own finances in some strange way.*

And here are two simple but essential rules about money that you should always remember to keep:

Rule No. 1 – Understand that money is spiritual, and it responds to spiritual laws..
Rule No. 2 - Don't forget rule No. 1.

Let me say this one more time, remember to pay yourself some reasonable percentage of your earnings, and budget for your necessary expenses and charitable giving, making sure that you discipline yourself to live within your means, and invest what you pay yourself to help you build a financial estate.

"A part of all you earn is yours to keep" Remember that. Now, to wrap it all up, let me say this again, money is spiritual and if you know how to manage it well spiritually, you will manage it well, physically too. I have an affirmation that I say every morning upon rising from bed and every evening before retiring to bed. This affirmation has helped awaken in me, the consciousness of abundance and wealth. I hope that it will resonate well with you too, and if it does, please feel free to make it your own.

Here it is:
I love myself; I like what I do, and I always do my best in it.

My work goes forth to bless, fill, inspire, elevate, and dignify the hearts and minds of men and women all over the world, and I have a lavish income consistent with integrity and mutual benefit.

Money is constantly circulating in my life, and I use it wisely, judiciously, and constructively. Money flows to me freely, joyously, and endlessly, and all my needs are met at every moment of time and point of space, and I have all sufficiency in all things, and I bound to every good work.

I have wisdom, riches, and wealth, I succeed in my endeavours, and I prosper in my ways. Divine law and order govern my life through divine Love, and I live a marvellous, and happy life. I am at peace, and it is well with my Soul.

Proclaim the above affirmation every day in the morning upon rising from bed, and in the night, just before retiring to bed, and declare it in faith and conviction (*If you don't have the conviction just yet, don't despair, it will come, just keep affirming the statement*). And if you keep at it, diligently, this affirmation will become part of your psyche and your reality, and in due course, it will manifest itself in your life, you'll notice some amazing and transformational results beyond your comprehension. Doors of opportunity will start opening before you, your imagination will feel so liberated so to say, and you will start having great and marvelous dreams of great and wonderful things to do.

It is all part of taking advantage of spiritual laws at work in the universe. All things are possible to those who believe.

And remember, your success is not a result of making money. Quite the contrary, making money is the result of your success, especially your success in developing yourself and in serving others. Your material success is in direct proportion to the service you render others. You can only legitimately earn money after you are successful. Success comes first. Most people, however, try to put it the other way around and thus spend a lifetime chasing after shadows.

Make yourself better every day, and make the service you render others excellent, and money will freely flow to you. That's how it works, don't chase after money.

For those of you who desire money and wealth, this is where our journey ends, and I thank you for your kind attention. I hope you learnt a lot and will be implementing what you have garnered from the preceding paragraphs of this chapter on MONEY And WEALTH.

For those of you who have amassed a lot of money but still feel like there is something missing, I have a question for you, and it is this:

Now That You Are Rich and Wealthy, What Next?

Well, you have done it! You now have the money, you have the connections, and you have the power. So, what's next for you? What is your next move? More riches? More wealth? More stuff? What are you going to do?

Here is what I have come to realise, when you amass wealth just for the sake of it, you will still somehow feel unfulfilled and lacking in something. And what on earth could that thing be?

Yap, you guessed it right, Meaning – the meaning of your life. You know that lingering question that sometimes keeps popping up in your mind, the – "*Is this it?*" Question. Yes, that one. That question is a signal to you that there is more to your life beyond the wealth, and riches you have accumulated, and the power you now possess.

And the truth is, there is no mysterious being who will come and announce to you that this is the meaning of your life or give meaning to your life. No, that's for you to decide, sometimes it is intuitive, you just know it, but at other times, for some people, it can be very difficult to discern, hence the emptiness, depression, and panic attacks that some rich, famous, and wealthy people tend to experience. And what I often recommend that you do under those circumstances, is take a spiritual odyssey to get to know yourself, deeply. Do enlist the help of a spiritual guide or teacher to take you through this odyssey should you wish to do so.

One of the things a spiritual odyssey will do for you is unshackle you from attachments to things material (or being materialistic), and it will also help you discover your true identity instead of deriving it from your wealth and riches.

And as you progress on this spiritual journey, your wealth and riches eventually then become just tools in your hands rather than parts of you. Knowing who you are will help you a great deal in authentically being true to yourself, and being down to earth enjoying everyday life, and not acting all that important, and thinking that you are above others. It will also help you to be relatable, to be approachable and loving, because you eventually come to understand that we are all, after all, one, having the same life, and that this life manifests itself differently.

Don't take yourself too seriously, enjoy the ordinary things of life - the rising and setting of the sun, the singing of the birds, the friendship and loyalty of a dog, the innocence of a child, the curiosity of a cat? Why not?

All I am saying is that, just be present, enjoy life in all its grand manifestations and take an active role in it.

Spending most of your time trying to act important or wonderful, or on the other hand being worried, afraid, or angry with others, won't do you any good. Use your wealth and riches the best way you can, as tools to build, to uplift and empower yourself and others, but not as tools for pride, arrogance, malice, and destruction.

Take your relationships seriously too. Have deep, and meaningful relationships that you are willing to be vulnerable in, because vulnerability is sign of trust, a sign of openness to life, a sign of willingness to become better. It is better than being superficial and stone cold. Open up, connect deeply from the heart and be human. You don't suddenly turn into a demigod because you have become wealthy. Remember, you still live on planet earth, a place uniquely designed for humans. So, be human, an enlightened human, if you will, and allow yourself to experience human emotions, the highs, the lows, and everything in between, enjoy the journey.

Being compassionate is also one of the other things that can really help give meaning to your wealth and riches. Helping to alleviate some of the pains, ills, and wrongs experienced by your fellow human beings who are trying to make ends meet. Being your brother's keeper as it were, in the best way you can, without necessarily taking over their burdens, but by just helping lighten the load.

It is my submission to you that if you consistently do the aforementioned things, there will be an abundance of meaning, fullness, depth, and richness in your life, and your being wealthy will be worth it.

Blessings to you.

> *Pay yourself not less than 10% from your take home pay. Remember, part of what you earn is yours to keep. No if's or but's, make it a rule.*

6

SEVEN ATTITUDES OF TRULY GREAT AND INFLUENTIAL PEOPLE

The keys to living a great and marvelous life are in your hands, and your attitude to life is the master key.

On one warm November day, many years ago, I was on a flight en-route to London Heathrow from Entebbe in Uganda, and I was seated by the window seat on that flight.

A couple of hours after take-off, we were flying over the Sahara Desert. The Sahara Desert is the largest in the world and occupies approximately 10% of the African continent. From the Atlantic Ocean in the West, the greater Sahara stretches across Africa to the Red Sea and down to the highlands of Ethiopia encompassing a whopping 9,100,000 square kilometres.

The Sahara is one of the hottest regions in the world with mean annual temperatures exceeding 30 degrees centigrade. In the hottest months, temperatures can rise over 50 degrees centigrade, and temperatures can fall below freezing in winter. The Sahara is extremely windy. Hot dust-filled winds create dust devils which can cause temperatures to rise even higher.

However, from this altitude of 36,000 feet above sea level, the Sahara does look really beautiful.

Anyway, I was kind of lost in my thoughts, admiring this beautiful scenery from 36,000 feet when suddenly, something caught my attention.

My eyes fell on the temperature readings on the small TV screen in front of me, and the temperature outside the plane was in negative.

What? Negative temperature? I blinked, then wiped my face with my hand as if to clear something off my eyes and I looked again on the screen. Oh yes, it was in negative!

Hang on, aren't we flying over the Sahara right now? A desert? One of the hottest places in the world? I asked myself. Yes, we are, came the answer almost immediately. So, why the freezing temperatures outside? I thought to myself.

In my sort of bemused state, I was just about to talk to my fellow passenger seated next to me (Tim), about this phenomenon when like light bulbs being switched on in my head, 'I saw the light'. What happened is that I recalled one of my geography lessons many years ago in school where I learnt that - the higher you go, the cooler it becomes.

Aaaah! I said to myself noddingly, hmmm..., now I get it! How true. Of course, I was 36,000 feet above sea level. It all makes sense.

Anyway, the unintended lesson I got from this momentary episode of the recollection of my geography lesson, was that; from a higher altitude, everything looks really wonderful and beautiful - even the deadly Sahara Desert!

You have probably heard it figuratively said that your attitude determines your altitude. In fact, the late Zig Ziglar - an American author, salesman, and motivational speaker, once said; "*It's your attitude and not your aptitude that determines your altitude*".

I agree, and that's what we are going to be talking about in this chapter - the attitudes for success in life, powerful attitudes of the great.

You see, the way you view life, people, circumstances and all the rest of it, depends largely on the altitude of your mind so to say, that is - *your thought frequencies and the level of how highly developed your thinking is.*

The altitude of your mind has a great impact on the attitude you manifest in life and vice versa.

The things that often stand between you and the achievement of your goals are;

i. The sort of plans you have made, and
ii. The attitudes with which you live your life. Your attitudes are really part of your belief system.

We have already talked about plans in previous discourses; we will focus on attitudes in this one.

The Concise Oxford English Dictionary defines attitude as "*a settled way of thinking or feeling*".

Your attitudes go a long, long way in determining what company of people you'll keep, what actions you'll take, how successful you will be in your career or business and above all, your attitudes, will determine when your plans will turn into reality.

Without actually realising it, some people fall short of incredible breakthroughs in their lives just because, their attitude to life and other people, is standing in their way. Your current attitudes are either helping you move forward or are making you lag in life.

The good news though is this, your attitudes are 100% under your control, and you can change them at any time, should you wish to.

Let's look at some of the attitudes that I believe can positively influence and empower you to make excellent progress in your life and achieve success. Great people have these attitudes.

1. Attitude of Gratitude

The online dictionary defines gratitude as the quality of being thankful, readiness to show appreciation for and to return kindness.

Gratitude is a wonderful thing to express. When you exude an attitude of gratitude for what people do for you, you make them feel important. The truth is, everything you say or do that causes another person to feel better in any way also causes you to feel better to the same degree. Haven't you realised that when you encourage, inspire, and motivate others, you feel motivated, inspired, and encouraged yourself?

And guess what?

The converse is true. When you degrade, insult and abhor anybody, you feel the same too!

The need for appreciation is a deep subconscious desire of every individual you meet. When you satisfy this need, you will, by all accounts, become one of the most popular people in that person's world, and the simplest way to express gratitude and appreciation is to simply say 'thank you (for whatever good they have done or said to or about you or others)' and mean it.

You can say thanks in a whole host of ways, like; giving compliments, expressing admiration, validating others, unconditionally accepting people for who they are, smiling at people, giving a hug or a pat on the back, etc. All these actions communicate one message; -well done 'buddy', I am really proud of you and thank you so much'.

Show people that you care, and mean it. Be grateful for the good things that happen to you and others.

In fact, one of the best ways to ensure your happiness is to assist others in experiencing their own. Those who bring sunshine to others cannot keep it from themselves, said James Banie.

2. A Forgiving Attitude

"Psychologists generally define forgiveness as a conscious, deliberate decision to release feelings of resentment or vengeance toward a person or group who has harmed you, regardless of whether they actually deserve your forgiveness.

Just as important as defining what forgiveness is, though, is understanding what forgiveness is not. Experts who study or teach forgiveness make clear that when you forgive, you do not gloss over or deny the seriousness of an offence against you.

Forgiveness does not mean forgetting, nor does it mean condoning or excusing offences. Though forgiveness can help repair a damaged relationship, it doesn't obligate you to reconcile with the person who harmed you, or release them from legal accountability".
Source:
https://greatergood.berkeley.edu/topic/forgiveness/definition

Jim Loehr and Tony Schwartz in their book; In the power of Full Engagement, said: "*The richer and deeper the source of our emotional recovery, the more we refill our reserves and the more resilient we become.*"

You see, people, almost invariably, are very emotional in the way they live their lives. They decide emotionally then justify logically. Emotions come first. Forgiveness to them is also an emotional thing.

When people are hurt, they become emotional, and for some, this leads to prolonged periods of anger, resentment, self-pity and being grumpy. Most people will justify these emotional states logically by saying that they are hurt. What they seem not to understand, however, is that a lot of their emotional energy which could otherwise be expended in some other productive venture is being put to waste on ruminating on the hurt feelings, instead of finding ways to heal from them.

It, therefore, stands to reason that the quicker they recover from any hurt, through total and sincere forgiveness, the better it is for them.

I know it is not easy to forgive, but I also know that it is difficult to have that full energy you need to put into achieving your goals if you are hurting and being resentful, because and angry and resentful state of mind is an energy guzzler and it will suck up most of your energy and you won't have much left for anything else. Forgiveness involves a process of healing first, the healing of your emotional wounds. I have talked about this in depth on the chapter 10 – How To Make a Powerful Comeback in Life on page 150, check it out.

So, if there is anyone you know out there who has hurt you in any way, whoever they are, please forgive them. It may be your parent(s), your spouse, your friend, your sibling, your pastor, teacher, workmate, it could be anyone really, it doesn't matter who they are, all I ask you to do is to find it in your heart the grace to forgive and release them from the pain they have caused you. I know it is not easy, but for your own sake, just do it. If truth be told, forgiveness is not really for the sake of the one who has offended you, no, it is for your own sake; for your own well being and restoration. You don't have to feel like forgiving someone for your forgiveness to be true or genuine. You just need to do it by the decision of your will, by pursuing activities or things that bring about healing to your soul from hurt feelings and the forgiveness will naturally follow as a consequence of healing. That is how true forgiveness can be achieved. You can't force forgiveness, it won't work. Forgiveness is a process that involves emotional healing on your part first, and whatever can help you heal emotionally from the hurt feelings, do that first before attempting to forgive whoever has hurt you.

However, your decision to forgive somebody does not in any way mean that you stop the legal system from taking its course. No. If what was done to you is criminal, and the law of the land through the criminal justice system is dealing with it, leave it to them, let the legal system take its course.
Your job is to heal, forgive and move on with your life.

Choose to heal and find forgiveness. Anger, resentment, bitterness, and revenge will only serve to alienate you from peace, happiness, and the good things in life.

3. Courageous Attitude

Here is the definition of courage from Wiki, it says; *"Courage (also called bravery or valour) is the choice and willingness to confront agony, pain, danger, uncertainty, or intimidation. Physical courage is bravery in the face of physical pain, hardship, death, or threat of death. In contrast, moral courage is the ability to act rightly in the face of popular opposition, shame, scandal, discouragement, or personal loss".*

Source: https://en.wikipedia.org/wiki/Courage

Courage is a very admirable quality. Your boldness will help you get as much as you need in life. The bold move makes you seem more confident and more powerful. More than that, the bold draw attention, and what draws attention, draws power. We just cannot keep our eyes off the audacious, can we? We can't wait to see their next bold move.

Most of us admire the bold and the bold are often honoured and celebrated. I have never heard or seen the timid honoured for their timidity, have you? But the bold are, and what's more, a courageous person is a forward and upward-looking person, he/she faces the future not with fear but with courage and determination, not with doubt but with faith.

The bold and courageous are willing to take great chances and reach for new horizons and remake the world around them. They recognise that there is more to their life than the ordinary day to day grind; they take the status quo and turn it around. It is simply magnetic and very inspiring to be around them.

The good news is that you can be one of these very brave ones yourself, be one of the bold and courageous ones of your generation.

Courageous individuals teach us to have our horizons limitless, and ultimately if we are to be true to our past (pleasant or unpleasant), we also have to seize the future every day, and it is courage that will be instrumental in helping us make the most of our time, abilities (effort), and opportunities as we pursue our goals in life.

And,

No matter how challenging life turns out to be, or how stony the road may become, courage enables us to persevere, not to falter or grow weary but to demand, strive and shape a better life for ourselves.

Just refuse to give up on the idea of the forward and upward move, and challenge yourself to accept nothing but ultimate triumph. And despite the most extreme odds you will get to face sometimes, in this journey of life, I encourage you to be strong, and bold, raise your confidence level high, and stand courageous, every day.

Don't be afraid.

"*Most fears are educated into us, and as such, they can also be educated out! Fear may be a lack of awareness of the presence of God as a real force in our lives. With the realisation of God's active presence in our lives, many aspects of fear may disappear into the mists of the unreal. Like a snowball dropped into a pail of hot water, fear dissolves, and its energy is transmuted into positive faith.*
As you begin to realise that God is lovingly in charge of your life, you may also understand that there is really nothing to fear" John M Templeton

A Compassionate Attitude

What is Compassion?
"Compassion literally means "to suffer together." Among emotion researchers, it is defined as the feeling that arises when you are confronted with another's suffering and feel motivated to relieve that suffering.

Compassion is not the same as empathy or altruism, though the concepts are related. While empathy refers more generally to our ability to take the perspective of and feel the emotions of another person, compassion is when those feelings and thoughts include the desire to help. Altruism, in turn, is the kind, selfless behaviour often prompted by feelings of compassion, though one can feel compassion without acting on it, and altruism isn't always motivated by compassion".
Source:
https://greatergood.berkeley.edu/topic/compassion/definition

Compassion makes you believable. It magnetises and magnifies the power of your faith and undeniably makes you very welcome and attractive in the eyes and hearts of many people.

Compassion bestows upon you the invisible power of influence and force of accomplishment.
Compassion naturally leads you to be a giver; it enhances the quality of benevolence - one of the hallmark characteristics of the truly remarkable people. When you give freely and generously of yourself to others or for a cause, you feel more valuable and happier inside.

Here is a principle to remember when it comes to benevolence and compassion: "The more you give of yourself to others without expectation of return, the more, good things there are that will come back to you from the most unexpected sources."

You will also realise that, over time, you'll start becoming more patient and understanding, less judgmental or demanding of others. You will feel peaceful, confident, and pleasant to be around. In a nutshell, you eventually become a better and finer person.

Isn't that wonderful? Embrace the attitude of being compassionate.

4. Integrity

The online dictionary defines integrity as "*the quality of being honest and having strong moral principles; moral uprightness*".

You see, your character is the most important thing that you develop in your entire life. True.
The hallmark of character is integrity, and you develop integrity, and become a sincere person, by practising telling the truth to yourself and others in every situation. Be true to yourself and to everyone around you. Of course, this does not mean that you will always be right 100% of the time in everything. It, however, emphasises the fact that you endeavour to tell the truth, as you see or know it, and tell that truth to yourself and the world around you.

Others will learn to know that they can confidently rely on you and your word (and that is very important in life). Though they may not like what you say on certain occasions, they will still know that you are always truthful, and this will go a very long way to earn you a great reputation in life.

In this day and age with the advancement of technology, CCTV and satellite, you cannot afford to be careless about how you conduct yourself or how you treat others or do business. To be successful nowadays is largely determined by the number of people who trust you and who are willing to work with you or give you credit if you are a borrower or help you during difficult times etc.

Trust is essential, and trust is earned not given, and you earn trust by being a person of integrity.

And more than that, being true to yourself is something you must never compromise.
Listen to what Shakespeare once said, "*To thine own self be true, and then it must follow, as the night the day, thou canst not then be false to any man*".

You must guard your integrity as a sacred thing, as the most important statement about you as an individual.
As Brian Tracy once said; "*Whenever you are in doubt about a course of action, simply ask yourself, is this the right thing to do? And then behave accordingly.*"

5. Attitude of Love and Generosity

What I am talking about here is that attitude of going the extra mile and doing a little bit more than you are expected or required to and not just doing the bare minimum.

It is that attitude of giving someone £11 when you could give £10, it's that attitude of saying thank you very much instead of just saying thanks, it's that attitude of getting up and giving a seat to that pregnant woman or senior on the train or bus when you really don't have to. Do you get what I mean? The attitude of being generous and loving.

Love and generosity go hand in hand, and you can't have one without the other for either of them to be meaningful and heartfelt by the recipient.

Be a Loving and Generous person. To love and to be generous are decisions you make by yourself, and they should form a core part of your life. Without genuine, heartfelt generosity and love for the people in your life and for the things you do, you risk living your life like an automaton, like a robot.

Is that the kind of life you want to live?

I hope not.

And remember, Love and generosity should begin at home. It is useless and in fact, questionable for you to lavish your love and generosity to other people while your family hardly receives any of it. That is not love and generosity, that is, in my opinion, showing off or being full of yourself, in other words, proud. And showing off or pride is something that a genuinely loving and generous person will fight, resist, and overcome, and will not tolerate in their life.

6. Humility

The human heart is full of pride, and therefore humility is not something that comes naturally to man.

The online dictionary defines humility as "*a modest or low view of one's own importance; humbleness*".

I don't think that in any way means that you should be going about degrading yourself and having a low view of yourself. No.

What I think it means is that you should be aware of how important you are (and it's true, you are important), but then, don't be full of yourself because of it. Neither do I think humility in any way means that you should be a doormat for people to walk all over you No, not in the slightest.

Humility is an attitude that you, yourself, decide to take upon. There is no such thing as forced humility. I think 'forced humility' as it were would best be called humiliation. And why do I say so, well, because humility is not about externals (appearances) but internals (character). You cannot force or fake character for long.

There is a statement I heard a long time ago, and it goes something like this; "a man convinced against his will is still of the same opinion". In other words, his heart is still the same; there is no change of heart.

Now, many of us I believe have had the experience of meeting people who are so full of themselves, people who think everyone should dance to their tune.
Honestly, how did you feel about being around such people? Did you feel like; yes, they are cool, I want to be like them? Or did you feel like beating *the hell out of them*?

I don't know what you felt, but I am sure you did not feel comfortable being around them. And that is precisely my point; when you are not humble but rather full of yourself, proud and arrogant, people will distance themselves from you. Most of those who will insist on being around you will do so for something you have, which they themselves want. But once they get it or once you no longer possess it, they will be off in a hoot.

Pride will hurt you in the end. It pays to be humble. So, be humble. Train yourself to be humble.

7. Positive Money Mindset

Truly great and influential people know the place money holds in life, and they take their financial life seriously. They are not frivolous or careless when it comes to money matters and they don't take chances where money is concerned. They value money, they don't think money or being rich is evil, or that having lots of money is the root of all evil. No, they don't believe such nonsense.

They understand that it takes money to do lots of things in this world, and they understand that they need to make money and be financially secure, independent and free.

Think of any great and influential person you know, and I bet you that all I have said in this section of a positive money mindset, applies to them, check it out for yourself.

So, if you want your life to be great and influential, having a positive money mindset will go a long way to helping you achieve that.

Now, while I encourage you to embrace the above seven attitudes, that is; being forgiving, courageous, compassionate, being a person of integrity, being loving and generous, being humble and being wealthy, I also implore you to keep your distance from the following twin attitudes: The **Entitlement attitude** and **Passivity.** For where you find one, the other is also bound to be there.

I wonder, have you ever met or had the unpleasant experience of interacting with a person who behaves as if the world owes them? They expect to be treated in a special way because of whatever they believe is unique about them.

I don't know about you, but I find it very challenging to be around such people. For most of the time, they are either showing off, or are grumpy, sulky, complaining, griping, accusative and downright annoying.

Nobody should go about laying claim on what someone else has worked hard for because they believe they are entitled to it. No, it doesn't work that way, absolutely not!

The entitlement attitude is toxic, and you should stay far, far away from it. It will alienate you from other people.

What you can do instead, is to work hard, be diligent and trust God within you to see you through your goals and aspirations. That's much better than thinking that you are entitled to a good life on the sweat of others.

A man should labour for himself and be a useful member of the community. And unless he has some sort of condition that makes it impossible for him to work, he should be ashamed to depend upon others for all he has, while giving nothing in return.

Passivity is the other negative attitude I recommend you never entertain in your life. Living your life passively is one of the surest ways of signing up to mediocrity and a life sentence of poverty and want.
You must be involved in what is happening in your life. Don't just be there and let things happen to you as if you have no say or intelligence to take an active role in how your life should be shaped.

Be an active player in shaping your own destiny, and don't be content on relying on hand outs.
If you live in an environment that restricts the pursuit of the goals and aspirations you have for yourself, then my recommendation is for you to change that

environment as soon as it's practicable and waste not even a second in that place. Get out of there as soon as you can, relocate somewhere else where it pays for you to exercise your inherent and inalienable right and authority to chart the course of your life.

If you are with someone who is a total pain, and one who is limiting your progress in life, think seriously about what you can do restrict their influence and impact in your life. And if that comes down to even ending the relationship, so be it. You shouldn't allow anyone to restrict your life to just mere existence when you have a lot to offer. You are meant to live life and live it to the full, not just exist and be noticed. Don't just go with the flow, determin the course you want to take and pursue it.

Being passive about life, and especially your own, is dangerous and must be avoided at all costs. There is no merit whatsoever in passivity, and you should watch yourself with a hawk's eye against this terrible, evil attitude of passivity.

Live your life and live it to the full. Be fully engaged in it and don't live as a victim. Take responsibility and take control.
I hope you will forever resolve to be a grateful, forgiving, courageous, compassionate, trustworthy, loving, generous, humble, and an assertive person, and be a force for good in your community, your country, and the world at large.

Thanks for your attention thus far. Let's now move on and consider the subject of self-acceptance next.

Without actually realising it, some people fall short of incredible breakthroughs in their lives just because, their attitude to life and other people, is standing in their way. Your current attitudes are either helping you move forward or are making you lag in life. The good news though is this; your attitudes are 100% under your control, and you can change them at any time, should you wish to.

7

THE MAXWELL MALTZ GUIDE TO SELF-ACCEPTANCE

Other people will love and treat you in direct proportion to how you love and treat yourself.

Self-acceptance is at the heart of every other good thing that will happen to you.

And I am not talking about dejected self-acceptance. No, I am talking about real, affirmative, positive, and unconditional acceptance of yourself and not looking for people's opinions to validate who you are.

One of the most valuable gifts you can give yourself is that of being true to yourself, being authentically you and living your life the best way you can, without pretending to be someone else or trying to please everybody. No pretence, no faking things in order to fit in, and certainly no pandering to people's opinions or ideas in order to feel validated. No, none of that, but just being yourself, and keep growing, and making the most of the best of you.

Never compare yourself to anyone else unless that person is the one looking at you in the mirror. And in that case, look them in the eye and say, hey, you look amazing today, and I love you, and you're going to rock your world today.

The greatest breakthrough and the greatest success in your life in my view is going to be self-acceptance. Self-acceptance is the springboard and catalyst for transforming your life to what you want it to be or look like.

The late Maxwell Maltz - an American cosmetic surgeon and author of **Psycho-Cybernetics,** articulated the subject of self-acceptance so well that I find it quite irresistible to defer to him and share with you what he had to say about self-acceptance.

He said: *"No real success or genuine happiness is possible until a person gains some degree of self-acceptance.*

The most miserable and tortured people in the world are those who are continually straining and striving to convince themselves and others that they are something other than what they basically are.

And there is no relief, and satisfaction like that comes when one finally gives up shams and pretences and is willing to be himself/herself.

Your 'self' right now, is what it has always been and all that it can ever be. You did not create it. You cannot change it. You can, however, realise it and make the most of what already is by gaining a true mental picture of your actual self.

There is no use straining to be somebody. You are what you are now.
You are somebody, not because you have made a million dollars or drive the biggest car in your block or win at the bridge - but because God created you in His Own Image.

Most of us are better, wiser, stronger, more competent - now than we realise. Creating a better self-Image does not create new abilities, talents, or power - it releases and utilises them. We can change our personality, but not our basic self.

Personality is a tool, an outlet, a focal point, of the 'self' that we use in dealing with the world. It is the sum of our habits, attitudes, learned skills, which we use as a method of expressing ourselves.

Self-acceptance means accepting and coming to terms with ourselves now, just as we are, with all our faults, weaknesses, shortcoming's, errors as well as our assets and strengths.

Let's admit to ourselves - and accept the fact that our personality, our 'expressed self' or what some psychologists call our actual self is always imperfect and short of the mark.

No one ever succeeds during a lifetime in fully expressing or bringing into actuality all the potentialities of the real self (Image of God). In our actual self – the expressed self, we never exhaust all possibilities and powers of the real self. We can always learn more, perform better, behave better.

The actual self is necessarily imperfect. Throughout life, it is always moving toward an ideal goal, but never arriving. The actual self is never static but a dynamic thing. It is never completed and final but always in a state of growth.
It is important that we learn to accept this actual self with all its imperfections because it is the only vehicle we have."
He further went on to say; "*We are engineered as goal-seeking mechanisms. We are built that way.*

When we have no personal goals which we are interested in and which mean something to us, we are apt to 'go around in cycles', feel 'lost' and find life 'aimless' and 'purposeless'.

We are built to conquer environments, solve problems, achieve goals, and we find no real satisfaction or happiness in life without obstacles to conquer and goals to achieve.
People who say that life is not worth living are really saying that they themselves have no personal goals which are worthwhile.

Always have something ahead of you to 'look forward to' - to work for and hope for. Look forward, not backward. Develop a nostalgia for the future.

In addition to your personal goals, have at least one impersonal goal to help your fellow man, not out of duty but because you want to.

I could not resist sharing those preceding wise words from Maxwell Maltz with you, and I hope you have found them very edifying, just as I did.

There is only one you; unique, fearfully, and wonderfully made. One of a kind, special. Fall in love with yourself, accept who you are from every vantage point and then watch the amazing transformation that will happen in your life.

Accept yourself and become your most ardent advocate and defender. No human being on earth will ever love you more than you love yourself, and I, therefore, advise that you become very practical and confident in the way you show yourself, love. For example, take yourself out, buy nice things for yourself, choose good friends for yourself, always talk positively about yourself, defend yourself against abuse and being taken advantage of, and take very good care of yourself.

You are unique, and you should embrace your uniqueness unapologetically, with grace and confidence. Accept yourself and be authentically you from every vantage point, and never apologise for being yourself.

If you treat yourself like a failure, or a nobody, don't be surprised when others treat you the same. The world has a way of mirroring back to you exactly what you are doing to yourself, even if you do it in secret.

So, every day, you have a choice to make, will you be true, loving, caring, and kind to yourself? Or will you be doubtful, unkind, feeling unworthy and defeated about yourself?

Whichever you choose, that's the one the universe will mirror back to you via other people, circumstances, and what is popularly called Fate. **You are the captain of your soul, the determinant of your destiny**.

8

WHO ARE YOU, AND WHAT ON EARTH ARE YOU HERE FOR?

A journey of self-discovery. A spiritual odyssey

If someone suddenly came over to you, said hi, and then proceeded to ask you this; Who are you? What would you say to them in response?

In fact, just sample out 100 people over the next ten days and ask each of them the same question: Who are you?

The typical response you will get will not vary much from the response below.

Most, if not all will say; I am ...... (their name or occupation).

But is that true? Does your name or your occupation tell us who you really are? I know the context in which that question is asked does matter, however, the truth of the matter is that identity crisis is one of the biggest crises in the world today. Most of us don't know who we really are.

Many people are searching for answers and trying out all sorts of things to try and understand who they are, what their purpose is, and how they can find meaning and fulfilment in life. In fact, it is not an exaggeration to say that no less than 95% of the human population is searching for answers to this fundamental question – Who am I, and what on earth are my here for? What is my purpose?

Now, on the subject of who we are, **Nikitas Stithatos** - a Byzantine mystic and theologian who is considered a saint by the Eastern Orthodox Church, said the following in the Philokalia volume 4. "*What I am is not at all the same as that which characterises me; nor is what characterises me the same as that which relates to my situation; nor is what relates to my situation the same as that which is external to me*".

In each case the one is distinct from the other in the following respects,

- *What I am is an image of God manifest in a spiritual, immortal, and intelligent soul, having an intellect that is father of my consciousness and that is cosubstantial with the soul and inseparable from it. This does not change.*

- *That which characterises me, and is regal and sovereign, is the power of intelligence and free will.*
- *That which relates to my situation is what I may choose in exercising my free will, such as whether to be a farmer, a builder, a cleaner, a doctor, and architect, an accountant, an entrepreneur, a mathematician, or a philosopher.*

- *That which is external to me is whatever relates to my ambitions in this present life, to my class status and worldly wealth, to glory, honour, prosperity, and exalted rank, or to their opposites, poverty, dishonour, ignominy, and misfortune.*

To know yourself in practice, therefore, means that you must guard yourself diligently from everything external to you; it means a respite from worldly concerns and cross-examination of your conscience.

In other words, things like; status, worldly wealth, poverty, prosperity, misfortune etc., should not define who you are, and you must make a conscious decision not to allow such things to define you.

Wise words, aren't they?

Another mystic and bible expositor, Neville Goddard, put it this way "*You are told that God became man that man may become God. You may think you are the man that God, as another, became, but I tell you: you are the God who became man, that man may become you! Because my visions which parallel scripture are accurate, I can boldly say that what I have just told you is true.*

In the 82nd Psalm we are the speaker, speaking to ourselves, saying: "I say, 'You are gods, sons of the Most High, all of you; nevertheless, you will die like men and fall as one man, O princes.'" We are the sons of the Most High, and we and our creator are one. Although we are now in a world of men, we have been promised that posterity will serve us and tell of the Lord who wrought it. You and I actually became human, that humanity may become spirit - as we are! You are not a little worm that God became. You were God before you devised the grand experiment, knowing it was the only way that man could become as you are!"

That is what Neville said. Quite interesting stuff, right?

And that sort of leads me to my next point contained in the following questions:

- What is my purpose in life?
- Why is there so much suffering in the world?
- Why are some people so rich and others very poor?
- Why are there so many religions in the world?
- Which God is the true God among all the Gods in the religions found in the world today?
- Why do good things happen to bad people and bad things happen to good people?

Have you ever asked yourself any of the above questions? If so, I think Neville Goddard might have an answer for you in a series of quotes below from his works.

"*You and your environment cannot be regarded as existing separately. You and your world are one.*

Therefore, you must turn from the objective appearance of things to the subjective center of things, your consciousness, and that is if you truly desire to know the cause of the phenomena of life, and how to use this knowledge to realize your fondest dreams.

In the midst of the apparent contradictions, antagonisms, and contrasts of your life, there is only one principle at work, only your consciousness operating.

Difference does not consist in variety of substance, but in variety of arrangement of the same cause-substance, your consciousness.

The world moves with motiveless necessity. By this is meant that it has no motive of its own, but is under the necessity of manifesting your concept, the arrangement of your mind, and your mind is always arranged in the image of all you believe and consent to as true.

The rich man, poor man, beggar man or thief are not different minds, but different arrangements of the same mind, in the same sense that a piece of steel, when magnetized, differs not in substance from its demagnetized state, but in the arrangement and order of its molecules. A single electron revolving in a specified orbit constitutes the unit of magnetism. When a piece of steel or anything else is demagnetized, the revolving electrons have not stopped. Therefore, the magnetism has not gone out of existence. There is only a rearrangement of the particles, so that they produce no outside or perceptible effect. When particles are arranged at random, mixed up in all directions, the substance is said to be demagnetized; but when particles are marshaled in ranks so that a number of them face in one direction, the substance is a magnet. Magnetism is not generated; it is displayed or manifested.

Health, wealth, beauty and genius are not created; they are only manifested by the arrangement of your mind – that is, by your concept of yourself [and your concept of yourself is all that you accept and consent to as true. What you consent to can only be discovered by an uncritical observation of your reactions to life. Your reactions reveal where you live psychologically; and where you live psychologically determines how you live here in the outer visible world].

The importance of this in your daily life should be immediately apparent.

The basic nature of the primal cause is consciousness.

Therefore, the ultimate substance of all things is consciousness." Neville Gordard – The Power of Awareness.
https://www.thepowerofawareness.org/chapter-two

"How successful you are on the outside is directly related to how relaxed you feel inside. Your emotional sense of well-being dictates your life." — Neville Goddard,
Relax More, Try Less: The Easy Path to Abundance

"Spiritual growth is the gradual, I would say, transition from a God of tradition to a God of experience."— Neville Goddard

"Assume the feeling of your wish fulfilled and continue feeling that it is fulfilled until that which you feel objectifies itself. If a physical fact can produce a psychological state, a psychological state can produce a physical fact. If the effect (a) can be produced by the cause (b), then inversely, the effect (b) can be produced by the cause (a). Therefore I say unto you, "What things soever ye desire, when ye pray, believe that ye have received them, and ye shall have them" (Mark 11:24, E. R. V.)."

"Imagination and faith are the secrets of creation." — Neville Goddard, Resurrection

"To attempt to change circumstances before I change my own imaginal activity is to struggle against the very nature of my own being, for my own imaginal activity is animating my world. If I believe that I am injured or that others are against me, I have conjured them in my world, and they have to be against me. If I fully believe that all are working towards the fulfillment of my good, they have to work towards the fulfillment of my good. I don't ask them. I don't compel them. I simply do it only within myself, and the whole vast world exists within me. Therefore, it is myself "pushed out." It's objectified. I don't have to change affairs; I only change it within myself, and then every one, though I know him or not by name, – it doesn't really matter, – it's myself "pushed out." — Neville Goddard, The Secret of Imagining

"The numberless unrealized hopes and ambitions of man are the seeds which are buried within the consciousness or virgin womb of man." — Neville Goddard, Your Faith is Your Fortune

"everything depends upon our attitude towards ourselves. That which we will not affirm as true of ourselves cannot develop in our life." — Neville Goddard, Be What You Wish

"He is in the world, and the world was made by Him, and the world knows Him not." — Neville Goddard, The Secret of Imagining

"You can't get away from your own imagination. You can't get away from it, because that's your own being. That is the reality. But it suffers with you. He is the Lord Jesus Christ within you. Now, test Him tonight. Test Him for the good. Do you want a better job when they say they are letting people out? Forget what the papers say. Forget what anything says. "All things are possible to the Lord Jesus Christ." (Matthew 19:26) If you don't have enough money, forget what the paper says, You assume that you have it. "All things are possible to God." (Matthew 19:26) He sets no limits whatsoever on the power of believing. Can you believe it? Well, try to believe it. Try to believe, first of all, in God. Well, God is your own imagination. Well, believe in Him; that whatever you can imagine is possible. Can you imagine that you have now the kind of a job that you want? The income that would come from it? The fun in the doing of the work? Well, then, walk as though it were true; and, to the best of your ability, believe that it's true. And that assumption, though denied by your senses, – though the world would say it is false; if you persist in it, it will harden into fact. This is the law of your own wonderful imagining. Believe it, and it will become a reality." — Neville Goddard, The Secret of Imagining

And in a talk he gave in the 60's, titled – **The Artist is God**. Neville said: "*God is the great artist, and there is no artistry so lovely as that which perfects itself in the making of its image. God has but one consuming objective, and that is to make you into His image, that you may reflect and radiate his glory. On this level, however, God exists as the human imagination, for the human imagination is the divine body called the Lord Jesus.*

On the highest level, God's great artistry is concentrated on the making of his image; on this level, he - as you - can do the same. A friend may say he would like to be a doctor; another friend wants to be a successful businessman or a dancer. Every desire is an image. As the artist, lowered to this level, you can form images of your friends. And if you persist in your assumption, in time, your friends will radiate and reflect your artistry.

God is the great dreamer in man, bound in a deadly dream until he forms the image called Christ, in himself. Only when Christ is formed in man will he awaken from his dream of life. Now, on this level, you can be bound in a dream, too. Perhaps you would like to be a great artist. That is your dream, your image. How would you feel right now if you were? Can you believe your assumption is true even though your reason and senses deny it? Can you persist in your imagination, as the highest level of your being persists in his image?

We are told: "When you pray, believe you have received it, and you will." Prayer is not a lot of empty words, but imagination braced in feeling. Every Sunday, people go to church, say the Lord's Prayer, and come out of the building just the same as they were when they went in. Their words were empty, as no prayer was answered. Now they are going to stop praying to their demoted mythological saints, for that is all saints are.

The most creative thing in us is to believe a thing into objective existence. Can you believe that something is already objective to you, even though your mortal eyes cannot see it? Can you walk, drenched in the feeling that it is an objective fact until it becomes so? That's how everything is brought into being, for all things exist in the human imagination, who is God himself.

Imagination is the divine body called Jesus, the Lord. If you are willing to step out, asking no one if it is right or wrong, and dare to walk in the assumption your image is true, it will come to pass...

Tonight I give you a principle: God is the great artist, who - as your own wonderful human imagination - is perfecting his work through the ages in the making of his own image in you. Do you have an image? Name it. Now, are you willing to simply assume that you have it, and wait for its objectification? Every image has its own appointed hour to ripen and flower. If it be long, wait, for its appearance, is sure and will not be late. Are you willing to wait for the happiness you now seek, or are you going to try to go on the outside and make it so? If you are willing to apply this principle and let it happen, you will become the successful businessman, doctor, minister, or whatever you desire to be. If you will assume your desire and live there as though it were true, no power on earth can stop it from becoming a fact, because you are God and your only opponent is yourself.

There is nothing but God, but man - not knowing this - creates opposition and calls it Satan or the devil, both of which are just as nonexistent as St. Christopher. Millions believe in them and give them power they do not possess.

But I urge you to believe in nothing but God, who is your own wonderful human imagination."
http://realneville.com/txt/the_artist_is_god.htm

When I first heard of Neville Goddard and his work, I was taken aback and surprised at the sort of things he was saying. You see, I was brought up in a Christian household and I was taught Christian tradition at a very early age. My great, great grandfather was an Anglican priest. However, What Neville says in his works is radically different, or so it seems, from most of the things I was taught about God, Jesus Christ, and Christianity at large. And what's more, he was teaching from the Scriptures, the Bible, and all that he was saying, were his interpretations of the scriptures, but in a very radically different way, a way that resonated with me. I kept being drawn to explore and listen to what he espoused on the subject of who we are and who God is. And all that information is still readily available on the internet and on YouTube.

I found and still find what Neville teaches quite fascinating and remarkable, and it will take a curious, thirsty, and an open-minded person to hear him out.

I will leave you to make up your own mind and draw your own conclusions about what Neville espouses if you ever happen to get hold of his talks and teachings. All I can say is that revelation is progressive.

And so, it comes as no surprise that my belief about God has somewhat evolved, and I would say this scripture in Ephesians 4:5-6 puts it right there at the centre for me, it says, "*There is one body and one Spirit, just as you were called to one hope when you were called; one Lord, one faith, one baptism, one God and Father of all, who is above all, and through all, and in you all.*"

There is only God, and nothing else. He is one and all. There is no other. He plays all the parts.

And the very fact that you may perhaps be wondering what the heck is he talking about, leads me to my next point - that of purpose, your purpose and destiny, and I believe it is this; to awaken to your true self, the God in you. That is your purpose and destiny - to become more Christ like, as the Christian faith puts it. And it is bound to unfold, regardless of the path you take to awaken, whether that be Christianity, Judaism, Islam, Buddhism, Hinduism, or many of the other paths practiced in the world today, or even if you don't practice any path at all. Let me try to illustrate it this way; imagine it is time for you to wake up in the morning, or after a nap or siesta during the day, it won't matter how you wake up, or what wakes you up, the important thing is that – you awaken from your sleep or nap. And so, it is, with spiritual awakening. It matters less which path, or way you awaken from, the important thing is that you awaken to who you really are, that's it. Whether that finds you as a Buddhist, Christian, Moslem, Jew, etc. And whether it takes one lifetime or many lifetimes, doesn't really matter, the awakening is what matters. I hope you get my point.

Now, you might find most of what has been said in this chapter to be quite esoteric, and I will understand if you find it hard to take it all in just yet. That's perfectly okay. For you see, there are levels and stages of growth, awareness, and experience in the physical world, and the same applies to the spiritual world too – there are spiritual stages and levels of growth, awareness, and experience. But ultimately, we are all moving towards the same destination.

Like I said earlier on, I was born into a Christian household and taught Christian values, I had no choice then, as a child, to choose my path. However, if I were to choose which religion to practice, now that I am an adult, I would still choose Christianity. Not because other religions are bad or wrong, but just because I am comfortable with Christianity. It's become part of my heritage, it is the foundation of most of my values, and my belief system was crafted on the back of Christian tradition. The Bible and the life of Jesus Christ have had an enormous impact in my life, and Christianity to me seems to be the path I will continue in, on my journey to spiritual awakening (enlightenment) and union with God, notwithstanding the fact that any of the other religions practiced in the world today, could well have been the path I would be following, was I to have been born into, and brought up, in a household that practiced any of those religions. So, I suppose it all depends on one's upbringing and how the religion practiced in their household influenced them while growing up. Or perhaps there was no religion practiced at all in your household, yet still, I believe there was some form of spirituality practiced, even atheists are spiritual.

I cannot at this stage of my spiritual journey endorse any religion or path, and neither can I in all honesty condemn any religion or path out there. I believe that religion is a way people choose to practice Spirituality, and Spirituality, in my view, is no religion, but a state of being or becoming. And we are all Spiritual beings, aren't we? But we manifest or express our Spirituality in many ways including - religion, art, music, literature, etc. And so, I believe that once you choose or find yourself expressing your spirituality under the auspices of any of the religions we have today in the world, for example, or no religion at all, it is important that you do not take it upon yourself to criticise or condemn someone else who has chosen to express theirs under the auspices of a different religion or way of being from the one you have chosen. Every religion has had its fair share of scandals and 'bad apples' and that doesn't make any of them bad or wrong. On the other hand, many of the major religions in the world have also done many good and wonderful things for humanity. The point I am making here, and one I hope you are getting is this; we are spiritual beings first, before we are human. Spirituality is our way of life, and I dare say, our only real way of life.

People practice spirituality in many, many ways, and every aspect of your life has a spiritual dimension to it that is helping to move you closer to a more perfect union with the divine – to oneness. It is my submission to you that, I believe there is nothing accidental or useless that comes to you or happens to you. There is nothing meaningless about your life, everything about you matters – whether that be good or bad as the human mind perceives it. Just pay attention and be present, become increasingly more and more aware and embrace the transcendent in you, and you will start noticing something quite remarkable about you. Everything you go through helps to shape and move you closer to the realisation of your true authentic self, what I call the image of God, as you awaken in ever deeper degrees of awareness. Every job you take, every business you start, every relationship you'll ever be involved in, everything you see, hear, and feel, plays a part in your spiritual journey. The challenge for you is to be fully present and take it all in and awaken.

Religion, politics, class status, nationalism, and many other associations including atheism, are all the various ways that people are trying to find themselves, and all of those things are all spiritual practices. We all somehow find ourselves in one of these things, however, *you need to transcend all of that, all associations and powers that may be, all identities, all dogmas, and all creeds, all religions and all else, and just come to pure unadulterated awareness, and there, you will find Yourself, which ironically, has always been there waiting for you*, just like the father in the parable of the prodigal son in - Luke 15:11-32, who was always looking out for the return of his son.

All those practices (*politics, religion, class status, nationalism, atheism, etc.*) are means to an end, and not an end in themselves. And that's why you need to transcend them. You shouldn't settle in, you need to go beyond them and cross the *veil of identity* and arrive home to oneness, where there is neither Greek or Jew, male or female, bond or free, rich or poor, but just, Being - *pure unadulterated awareness of the unity of all*. In the Christian faith, I believe this is referred to as oneness in Christ, Christ being the invisible image of the invisible God. And this epignosis if well understood, liberates the Soul from bondage to things sensual and temporal, and lifts one to unparalleled wisdom of divine realities.

9

HOW TO FORM MEANINGFUL AND MUTUALLY BENEFICIAL RELATIONSHIPS

The secret to having great relationships.

Your great moments and your worst moments in life will one way or the other be directly related to the relationships you are involved in. Relationships do offer solace, they offer nurturing, support, and fun. However, they are also sometimes the source of distress, frustration, and deep despair.

In this world of human interconnectedness, relationships are like the oxygen that sustains our breathing. Someone once said that 'relationships are everything'. So true, I agree, 100%.

Over the course of your life, you will form many relationships along the way. Some of them will be deep, and some will be shallow. Some will be serious, and

some will be causal, and all of them, will play a part in the way you'll experience life.
There are many different types of relationships, and the common ones are Family relationships, Friendships, Acquaintances, Business relationships, and Romantic relationships.

Relationships just don't happen on their own (even family ones), they have to be formed and once formed, they need to be natured or maintained well.

What I would like to share with you in this chapter, are some principles I believe will enormously be helpful in forming and maintaining great relationships, regardless of the type of relationship it is. Call them your standards or principles of great relationships if you will. For you see, great relationships won't fall from heaven, you'll make them here on earth, and you've got to play your part in forming and naturing or maintaining those great relationships you want.

Some relationships are easy to form, and some aren't. The principles I am going to share with you will help you with both, and doing so without stressing yourself out, and actually, kind of enjoy doing so.

I have to say from the very onset that in forming relationships, rely more, but not exclusively, on your head (logical part of your being) than on your emotions (the emotional part of your being). More on that later. For now though, trust me when I say you should rely on your head, I know what I am talking about, you will save yourself many days of wondering what the hell happened, and also save yourself tears of being heart broken.

let's get started.

To begin with, if you want to form great relationships in your life, get to know yourself intimately and decide exactly what you want and what you don't want in the relationship you are about to establish or desire to establish.

You see, many people in our world nowadays don't really know who they are, or what they want, and I suspect it's because they are in the imitation game. They are trying so hard to live other people's lives that they completely forget to live their own. Sometimes they do so consciously, but often, unconsciously. They have not taken the time to get to know themselves. That's the problem.

They don't know or understand why they do some of the things they do, and they have vague ideas as to what makes them really happy. More often than not, they tend to be swayed so much in their thinking by the mass media. They let the media and public opinion do their thinking for them.

Really! Wow! Unbelievable. I used to be one of those people until when I had an awakening and understood who I am. Everything has changed since then, for me. I now have my own mind, and I make my own decisions, and I live my life, my way. Not in a braggadocious or arrogant manner, but just the way I like it. My life is beautiful now, many times over, and I love it.

Look, if you don't take time to know yourself and decide on the kind of things you'd like in your life and relationships, based on your knowledge of yourself, you are more likely to start on the wrong footing and end up with some things you'll not particularly want in the long run.

So, it will help a great deal for you to have a written down idea of what exactly you want, it just keeps your mind focused and not wandering about aimlessly.

Get to know yourself well, and based on that knowledge of yourself, develop a list of your non-negotiables. Sometimes, to get a better understanding of what you want in a relationship, it's best to inform yourself on what you don't want. Figuring out immediately all the things you want can be a bit tricky, but, usually, you know exactly what you don't want almost instantly. So, sit down and put together a list of criteria that would disqualify a potential match for a relationship, do that first. Get those criteria down on paper as your non-negotiables.

On the opposite end of the non-negotiables criteria, or on the flip side of the page, write down those things you like and are comfortable with and don't mind having in your relationship.

Don't rush this first step, and I seriously mean that, don't rush it. If it's going to take you six months to a year to do it (especially if you are thinking of a marriage relationship), so be it. But don't rush it. I can almost hear you say, Whaaaat! And my answer is Yeeees, exactly, no rushing.

That's principle or standard number one.

Secondly, now armed with the knowledge of who you are and what you want and don't want in the potential relationship, it's now time to go out there and start looking for the right person, and also get ready to screen out those who get attracted to you, screen them out to find out those who could be a potential match.

I told you, great relationships are made, they are not ordained. You have to look around. Some of the potential candidates will be drawn to you, and you will be drawn to some of them. There will be a variety to choose from. Not everyone will be a fit for you, and you will have to pick and choose.

Now, I want to digress abit and say this; be careful about rushing to establish relationships because someone has told you that there is somebody, they know, who is God-ordained for you. No, don't fall for it.

Unless that same God has spoken to you too, in a way you know how, don't believe such nonsense. Don't get me wrong here, I do believe in God, but in the one who dwells in me, dwells in you, and in everything. The almighty God, not some pseudo god who leaves me out of the picture of things that concern me. No, not that god.

So, be careful about this God stuff in relationships, unless you can confirm it within yourself that what the other person is saying sits well with you too, well, don't fall for it in the name of God. Many people have entered into relationships in the belief that "they are obeying God' and they are now living in 'hell' so to say. Don't become a statistic too.

Okay, back to the subject, you've now narrowed your search to two or three people, and it's now time to get to know them a bit more closely. Read on.

Once you start seeing other people with a view to establishing a relationship with them, there are some great principles for relationships I have come across and used in my life that can really be of enormous help to you at this stage, and the burden of the rest of this chapter is to try to shed light on these principles, and in doing so, I trust you will be able to understand and appreciate your relationships better, and thus enhance and enrich them – make them great.

For relationships to be great and successful, they must be **defined** and kept defined.

Now, when I talk about defining a relationship, what exactly do I mean?

What I mean is this:

- *It is about establishing clarity on the purpose of the relationship you are in or one you are seeking to get in to.*
- *It's about making sure that you both understand why you are in the relationship you are in, and*
- *Defining your relationship also includes being willing to do your part to make the relationship a success, that is - pledging your commitment, and allegiance.*

You see, **Where the purpose of anything is not understood or known, abuse is often inevitable,** and relationships are no exception to this reality.

And if truth be told, many people, sadly, have abused or are abusing their relationships, and are thus betraying the trust of those who have given them the wonderful privilege of being in communion with them in those relationships.

The inevitable consequence of such abuse is that many of the victims now find themselves hurt, betrayed and lonely, with the culprits hopping from one relationship to another, and all for the wrong reasons and causing many heartbreaks.

Protect yourself from such people, and better still, don't be one of them.

And so, here for your consideration, are some guiding principles you can use to define and govern your relationships.

1. The first principle is **Honesty**

When it comes to relationships, the sooner you set things straight, the better. Set things straight with yourself and with others.

When meeting people and seeking to establish relationships with them, be honest about your intentions. Be transparent and forthcoming about your expectations and the contributions you will make to the relationship.

By being honest, you set a strong foundation for the relationship you intend to pursue and at the same time, you would have avoided getting into a fake relationship - one based on ambiguity and possibly deception. Demand honesty in all your relationships. Do not entertain lies and deceit in any of your relationships, however cutely those lies come by.

HONESTY is the best policy. Be honest or true to yourself first, then insist that the person you are seeking to enter into a relationship with do the same. In that way, you will be coming from a place of understanding and openness, rather than one of uncertainty and secrets, which will more than likely cause big problems in the relationship and even destroy it later on.

2. The second principle is to **Know Thyself.**

We have already talked about this earlier on in this chapter, but let me talk about it here as a principle for defining and maintaining great relationships.

"The saying 'Know thyself ' may refer by extension to the ideal of understanding human behaviour, morals, and thought, because ultimately to understand oneself is to understand other humans as well. However, the ancient Greek philosophers thought that no man can ever comprehend the human spirit and thought thoroughly, so it would have been almost inconceivable to know oneself fully. Therefore, the saying may refer to a less ambitious ideal, such

as knowing one's own habits, morals, temperament, ability to control anger, and other aspects of human behaviour that we struggle with daily". (Wikipedia)

Now, isn't it interesting that some people, once they get into relationships, tend to want to change everyone else in the relationship but themselves? It's not difficult to understand why this happens; If one fails to take time to know themselves, almost invariably they will fail to recognise and appreciate others for who they are, and hence the effrontery to want to change others.

News flash - You cannot change anybody. Forget it. Change always begins with an audience of one - YOU! You initiate the change you want to see and muster the courage to see it through. Others will change themselves if they want to and when they are ready to do so. You can't force them to, you've probably tried it already.

In talking about knowing thyself, I am obviously under no illusion to suggest that you will be able to know yourself fully, no, not in one lifetime.

"In the true theological sense, 'Know Thyself ' is a fundamental tenet of the question of life's meaning. To truly 'know oneself' in this sense involves a deeply personal, spiritual transformation whereby a person would seek to orient themselves towards understanding their own phenomenological perceptions of reality, so as to gain earnest insight into aspects of one's own existence". (Wikipedia)

Let's make it simplistic by saying this; at least you

can know your core life attributes and align yourself with such virtues like; truth, prudence, patience, love, justice, and forgiveness.

And more than just aligning yourself with them, you can decide to go a step further and practice them! Ever heard of the phrase; "Walk the talk"? become a better version of yourself, and live out your true authentic self, at all times.

3. The third principle is: **do your due diligence**

Here is a bit of advice; whenever somebody wants to pursue a relationship (of whatever nature- personal, business or otherwise) with you, make it your responsibility to do your due diligence on them – check them out before committing yourself. Avoid just falling into relationships. It is worth taking time to have a healthy scepticism and do your due diligence.

It is incumbet upon you to sas out how honesty and integrity of the other person you want to establish a relationship with. The scripture says in 1 Thessalonians 5:21 (KJV); that, "*Prove all things; hold fast that which is good.*"

I would recommend that you take the time to understand what the other party is seeking and bringing to the relationship before signing up to it.

Remember, the onus is on you to be responsible for your life. You do your due diligence, not so much as to find fault with the other party, no, but to establish *credence and the strength of their character.* How credible is the person in question, and what is their propensity to stay so in the long term? That is what you are trying to establish during your due diligence work.

Check out what their **values and beliefs are, learn about their flexibility in life. What understanding do they have of the purpose of the relationship they seek to establish with you? What are their plans for the future, and are they capable of embracing change when it happens, or will they freak out?** Find out as much information as possible, and make sure you understand what you are getting into before committing yourself to the relationship.

Doubtless, you will find some unpleasant things/issues about people's past and whatnot. It would, however, be a terrible indictment to your sense of fairness if you were to rule out somebody purely based on their past mistakes. This is because mistakes don't and should not define anybody; we all have made and will make mistakes, and the truth is, some people do genuinely change. So, don't just write off somebody because you have seen some dirt in their past. How are they now? That's the important question.

However, if during your due diligence, you find no evidence of any apparent change in their character or behaviour, then I suggest you'd better tread your next steps carefully or not get involved at all.

You will be amazed at what this process (due diligence) can help you accomplish in terms of making decisions.

I dare say that there are people currently in relationships, who said YES when they should have said NO, because they did not do their due diligence, and they are now regretting their decision.

And there are those who said NO when they should have said YES, also because they did not do their due diligence, and as such have missed out on a very, very great relationship. So true, no doubt.

Anyway, do your due diligence and do it properly. Keep emotions out of the way, and when you finally come to say YES or NO, it will be an emphatic and a well-informed YES or NO.

Maintain this process of due diligence throughout the course of your journey together in the relationship. You do so, to investigate rumours and all sorts of things that will be thrown at your relationship. Rumours can destroy relationships if not properly investigated and dealt with.

4. Commitment to one another and to the relationship is the fourth principle

Once you've decided to enter into a relationship in good faith, the next best thing to do is to make a total commitment, in your heart, to make that relationship work. Pledge your full allegiance to it and to one another. Listen to one another, don't trash each other.

Many relationships fall apart because either one or both parties in it have not fully committed themselves to it and to one another in the relationship.

The greatest tests of people's commitments to each other and to their relationships are life challenges and troubles. When troubles ensue in a relationship, you will often find that the uncommitted party(s) are quick to run away, or 'jump ship' as it were, and thus killing the relationship all together, and in the process, breaking the heart of the other person who was commited.

What you must understand is that a relationship is an entity in its own right, and it needs nurturing and care.

Commit to the relationship by committing to one another, because the relationship is non-existent without either of you.

I would like to believe that any relationship you get into should serve a purpose bigger than you and that it should benefit all concerned.

When your relationships start being just about you, that's it; you have lost the plot. It starts getting toxic from that point on. Your relationships should never, ever, be only about you as an individual, and neither should they be about everyone in the world, but they should be about the common good, goals, and aspirations of those in it. Those who have formed it and are part of it.

If your relationship(s) is to serve your common needs, it will require care, attention and protection by those in it, from those outside of it, who want to destroy it.

You, therefore, need to be the guardians of your relationship and fight off anything and anyone who would want to destroy it.

So, if you don't want your relationships to struggle, endeavour to keep the big picture in mind – the big picture, in this case, is looking at the survival and viability of the relationship and working to make sure that the relationship serves both of your interests and that you are committed to one another and to making it work.

5. Fifth, **let your YES be YES, and your NO be NO**

If you want your relationships to thrive, then make sure there is no room for second-guessing your words and actions. You must communicate clearly and comprehensively where necessary.

Poor communication almost invariably creates problems in relationships. The way people talk (or don't talk) to one another sometimes causes lots of distress and tension.
For example, a domineering, demanding, intrusive communication will serve to cause one party to pull away or not communicate in return.

On the other hand, parties not showing any concern or empathic understanding by not responding to their partner physically or emotionally can also cause a break in communication with very unpleasant consequences.

If you are not sure of anything, simply say; *' I can't comment on that right now, can I get back to you on that?'*

then go, think things through carefully, and get back to the other person with your response.

6. And here is the sixth principle; **Operate under Love and Forgiveness**

These two factors are essential in any relationship, both at its inception and in its lifetime.

None of us is perfect, and we are bound to annoy others in relationships. It happens.

The truth is, we get things wrong more often we care to admit, and that is why there should be scope for forgiveness in your relationships, and the forgiveness should be motivated by love; for Love covers a multitude of sins, scripture tells us – *1Peter 4:8.*

Here is what Jesus Christ said – "*Love the Lord your God with all your heart and with all your soul and with all your mind. This is the first and greatest commandment. And the second is like it: 'Love your neighbour as yourself. All the Law and the Prophets hang on these two commandments.*" - Matthew 22:36-40

Those two commandments perhaps sum up all that I have been saying throughout our time together in this chapter.

I don't see how any relationship can be holistically sustained without love and forgiveness being the bedrocks and foundation on which it is built and sustained.

One of the reasons we should seek to forgive others is in order to gain control of our lives from hurt emotions.

Now, what if you don't feel like forgiving, what can you do?

Well, true, there are times when you feel like not forgiving, let alone even lay your eyes on the person who has hurt you or wronged you.

Forgiveness, however, is an act of your own will. You have to make a choice whether to forgive or not to forgive someone who has wronged you. But bear in mind that, choosing not to forgive others fosters bitterness and resentment. And bitterness has been linked to stress-related illnesses by some medical professionals. We don't know the whole mechanics of how that happens, but I believe there is much truth in it. By forgiving others, we free ourselves emotionally and spiritually. And it is best to have no preconditions in the decision and act of forgiveness.

When wronged, forgive and trust God to bring about your emotional healing. He is faithful and will surely do so.

Remember that two wrongs cannot make a right. What I mean is this; if someone does something wrong to you, you don't have to equally do a wrong thing to them to make it even. That won't make it right, would it? Of course not.

Said another way; you shouldn't start doing the wrong thing because someone else has stopped doing the right thing, and neither should you stop doing the right thing because someone else has done or has started doing the wrong thing.

7. Seventh principle - **Review your relationships from time to time**

The truth is that we all tend to deviate from our best intentions from time to time, and that is quite normal.

What is not acceptable, however, is first of all, the failure to realise or recognise when you have drifted, and secondly, the failure to make the necessary adjustments or amends if and you've realised that you have strayed.

That is why reviewing your relationships from time to time will help you **make the most of your relationships** - ***Define them and keep redefining them*** so that they continue being relevant in serving your common purposes in changing times.

That's it from me for now on how to form meaningful and mutually beneficial relationships. In the next chapter, we will look at how to bounce back from mistakes, setbacks, and disappointments in life. It makes for an interesting and uplifting read. See you there.

> *Commit to the relationship by committing to one another, because the relationship is non-existent without either of you.*

10

HOW TO BOUNCE BACK FROM MISTAKES, SETBACKS, AND DISAPPOINTMENTS IN LIFE

When you know better, you do better. So, stop putting yourself down over past mistakes. Do better now, now that you know better.

Mistakes, setbacks and disappointments happen, and no one is immune or exempt from them. A friend or relative of yours could be going through a very, very tough time right now because of some mistake they've made, or because of a setback, or disappointment they are dealing with. Or it might be closer to home, perhaps it's you who is having a tough time right now because of, you know, some mistake you've made or because of some setback or disappointment you are dealing with currently.

How can you successfully bounce back in life and get back on track in your life after a mistake, setback, or disappointment happens to you?

That's exactly what I would like to share with you in this chapter. I have some tips and ways of successfully dealing with mistakes, setbacks, and disappointments when they happen in your life.

So, first of all, like I said before, mistakes, setbacks, and disappointments happen, and nobody is immune, or exempt from them. We all make mistakes, we all experience setbacks, and we will all meet with disappointments many, many times in our lifetimes.

"To make no mistakes is not in the power of man, but from their errors and mistakes, the wise and good learn wisdom for the future." Plutarch (46 AD – 120 AD)

So, for starters, don't be so hard on yourself or others when mistakes happen, and don't take things personally either when you meet with a disappointment or experience a setback as you try to make the most of your life.

To a great extent, we humans are adventurous, we like to explore, and as such, in our quest to enjoy, to learn, to grow, to discover and develop ourselves, we will sometimes inadvertently take detours, and in so doing, we will occasionally hit 'dead-ends'. It happens.

So, when stuff happens like that, and you hit a dead-end because of some silly mistake you've made, don't beat yourself up, or give up and wallow in despair. Instead, get yourself together, and find a way out, and keep moving forward.

You need to have the courage and fortitude to go

forward despite your shortfalls or shortcomings. Don't lose sight of that glorious, and bright future ahead of you, despite the immediate darkness you might be experiencing right now.

Your mistakes, or other people's mistakes should not define you, and neither should you allow anyone or anything to bring you down because of them. Instead, choose to live your life with hope, with courage, with faith, with purpose, and conviction. And when you make a mistake, or experience a setback or disappointment along the way, here is how to make a comeback, or bounce back.

The first thing to do is to **acknowledge** it when it happens and come to terms with the fact that it is what it is.

What do I mean?

What I mean is this; if you make a mistake, or experience a setback, or if someone has disappointed you, acknowledge what has happened, and don't try to deny it and behave as if nothing has happened. There is no meaningful progress you will make in coming out of your predicament if you choose to deny or keep denying the fact that you have made a mistake or have had a setback, or have been disappointed.

It will serve you better to come to terms with your situation. Will it make things worse? I don't really know. Maybe it will, maybe not. But what's for sure is this; the cost of denial and not owning up to your mistakes or coming to terms with what has happened in your life, will be very, very expensive, in the long run.

Remember this though; coming to terms with something does not necessarily mean settling for it. No, that's not what it means. What it means is that you recognise and acknowledge that what has happened has happened, and see it for what it is; a mistake, setback or disappointment.

So, if you have made a mistake, come to terms with the fact that you have screwed it up, and own up to your mistake. Or if someone has messed you up, recognise that fact and come to terms with it. Only and only then will anything you do about your situation, start to make sense, and in so doing, you will be in a better position to bounce back well without any or much psychological damage to yourself.

Secondly, resist the temptation to start labelling blame (and that includes blaming yourself) for whatever mistake, setback, or disappointment you experience in your life. Blaming has never solved problems. What you need to do is take 100% responsibility for the outcome you now desire to see, and start right away where you are, to work on the getting to that outcome.

However, if what has happened to you is something you need to report to the authorities, by all means, go ahead and do so. Perpetrators of violence and danger to others should face the justice system to stop them from hurting other people. What you should avoid doing, when someone has messed you up, is taking matters into your own hands to avenge yourself. Don't do that, leave it to the legal system and rather focus most of your energy on recovery, and forward motion to your goals and aspirations.

Focus on:

- finding solutions to your challenges,
- fixing any problems you can, and
- moving on with your life.

That's what you should do.

The third thing to do to make a comeback is to develop a habit or the attitude of **never taking anything personally**. I repeat, don't take whatever happens to you personally. Instead, adopt a scientific approach to your situation. You know, Scientists, have very curious minds; they investigate, analyse and draw appropriate conclusions. Be like them in looking at your situation.

Understand that setbacks, mistakes, and disappointments are all effects. All of them have causes somewhere, and I suggest that you endeavour to find out what the real causes of your mistakes, setbacks and disappointments are. I know it is not easy to do what I have just suggested, especially when you are in the mix of emotions, and feel like everything is falling apart. I've been there before myself, several times, and yes, it is not easy. But if you want to sort yourself out, then you must sit back, try to relax, and reflect on what is happening in your life with a view to finding out the fundamental cause(s) of your problem(s). This is what I call self-reflection.

I implore you to give it a try, and many more try's if you don't succeed in the first instance – try to understand the cause(s) of your predicaments in life. Over time, you will come to appreciate what a powerful tool self-reflection and analysis is.

Looking for the causes of the challenges you face in life and having an inquisitive mind will help you not only to bounce back quickly from your setbacks, mistakes, or disappointments, but it will also make you wise.

So, *don't take things personally. Take the view that, whatever happened, did not happen to you but -* ***for you.*** Investigate it, and learn what you can, and move on with your life; stronger, wiser, and better equipped for the next challenge that may come.

There is one thing I want to touch upon here before moving on to the next point. It is related to an aspect of decisions and outcomes, and I feel you should be aware of this thing.

It is this; you have control over the decisions you make and actions you take, but hardly do you have control over the outcomes of those decisions and actions. Once done, it is done. Outcomes have probabilities built into them, and as far as I know, nobody has control over probabilities. The outcome can go either way.

You might make a very wise and sound decision and take the appropriate action about something, and then things work out in a totally different way than you anticipated. For example, circumstances might change along the way and thus totally affect the outcome you hoped for. Should you then blame yourself for that? Really? Of course not. You did your very best, and things just turned out otherwise. You didn't mean to do the wrong thing. Do you get my point? I hope you do.

So, keep making those good decisions and taking those right actions, and don't be put off by offside outcomes. Yes, you might be disappointed or even experience setbacks, but you must not give up. If things don't turn out as expected, don't beat yourself up and get all depressed and sad about it. Make another decision to counter the setback or disappointment and carry on living your life.

Don't take the result of the outcomes personally either, especially if they are not in your favour. The unexpected sometimes happens, and it doesn't mean you should get all so depressed and downcast. No.

Moving on, **the fourth** thing in your list of things to do to aid you in your comeback after a mistake, setback or disappointment is to find it in your heart to forgive all concerned. Yes, that's right. It is in your own best interest to exercise your inalienable right to forgive all those who have done you harm in the past, present and future. Mistakes and disappointments never happen without someone being hurt in the process.

The quicker and sooner you forgive yourself, and all those concerned the swifter and faster your bounce back and recovery will be.

When you are deeply hurt, forgiveness can sometimes be a very, very difficult thing to contemplate. I get it.

The truth is, in life, you will be hurt, that's for sure, it happens, and you can't decide not to be hurt when you experience something hurtful. However, remaining hurt, or being healed of the hurt feelings is a choice you have to make. Healing is a process of which forgiveness is a sign that you have healed. Focus on the healing process (self care, renewing your mind, personal development), and before long, you will arrive at forgiveness. One thing is for sure though, and that is, you can't force forgiveness, and don't even try to do it. Like I have said before, forgiveness is a point you arrive at, after a process of healing (in your soul) from hurt.

Trying to forgive before you are healed won't really work. And please note that healing can be instantaneous, or it may take a while. In any case, focus on getting healed, and forgiveness will not be an issue. And when you are hurt, don't suppress your hurt feelings, acknowledge them, and find a way to express them. You can do so by talking to somebody you trust, for example, or a by talking to a therapist, etc. The act of talking to somebody you trust about the hurt feelings you are experiencing, will help you heal faster and thus hasten the arrival of the point of forgiveness.

Remember, we all make mistakes, and we all deserve forgiveness.

The fifth comeback idea I can give you is to get busy working on your goal(s). Don't stay idle. Have you ever heard of the phrase - "*an idle mind is the devil's workshop*"? I think there is much truth in it.

Anyway, keep yourself occupied with something worthwhile and avoid idleness. And neither should you entertain thoughts of self-pity, regret, or revenge.

If you keep yourself, both mind and body busy involved in edifying activities, and in the company of supportive people, it will help you to recover and bounce back a lot faster. Don't isolate yourself or spend your time in the company of non-supportive and negative people. Got it? Good.

The sixth one is particularly to do with setbacks, and it is this; when you experience a setback in something you are persuing, be patient, but don't become complacent. Be patient with yourself and with others concerned and keep your eyes on the goal. There is no point in getting all too angry and frustrated over the setback. I heard it once said that "a setback is a set up for a comeback". It is a good way to look at it.

The seventh thing I can recommend you do to bounce back from a mistake, setback, or disappointment is to seek and ask for help.

You might be in need of financial help, emotional support or just reassurance from time to time that things will be just fine. Whatever it is you need, ask for it. By not asking for help or support when needed, you short-change your opportunities for healing and recovery. You'll continue to live in pain and anguish when things could otherwise be different and better, and to be honest, most of the time, if you don't ask for help, you are the one who will ultimately suffer the most.

There are times in our lives when we will inevitably need the help and support of others. The question is, will you ASK for it?

If you know somebody who can help you, go and ask them for the help you need. Don't let pride or fear hold you back. Don't suffer in silence, go get help.

Just be aware, however, that some people will not give a second thought about what you are going through because of the mistakes you've made, and some might even insult you or call you names. But whatever happens, let it not deter you from seeking the help and support you need to bounce back.

When you meet rude and unpleasant people who will be quick to criticise and condemn you for your mistakes like they never make mistakes, don't take it personally. They have no clue what you are going through, so, resist the temptation to get back at them, instead Just focus your energy and attention on getting help. I am confident someone, somewhere, somehow, will give you the support you need if you don't give up or despair. Remember, you are not your mistakes. Mistakes don't make you, you make them, and it doesn't mean you are them because you made them. And besides, you can turn your mistakes and disappointments into something that can work in your favour by adapting an optimistic and faith filled attitude in life. You must keep that distinction between who you are, and your mistakes very clear; otherwise, you run the risk of affecting your mental health.

It is also worth noting that there is no mistake too big that the grace and love of God can not cover!

And the God I am talking about is not a God afar off somewhere in the milky way, but one who is the very essence of your being, one who is always with you no matter what. He has promised never to leave you nor forsake you and you can count on him at any time.

Jesus Christ declared that "*I and my father (God) are one*" John 10:30. And I am also reliably informed from the scriptures (Hebrews 2:11-13) that *Jesus is not ashamed to call them brothers!* And who are these brothers? You and me of course! Us. Do you understand what that means? Wow! What a marvelous revelation. When you grasp that, you will be able to successfully deal with any challenge in your life and bounce back quickly. Scripture says in Isaiah 59:1 '*Behold the Lord's hand is not shortened that it cannot save; neither his ear heavy that it cannot hear.*'

Now is the time to arise and shine! Every day is a brand-new day full of potential and opportunities to start all over again. There isn't any merit whatsoever in living a defeatist lifestyle because of the mistakes you have made or setbacks and disappointments you have experienced or are currently experiencing. The truth is, there is a lot more still ahead of you to savour and enjoy than there is behind you to wallow in self-pity and regret. See the story of Joseph in the old testament of Bible, from a prisoner to prince and ruler, *you can find that story in the book of Genesis chapters 37 -50.*

A word is enough for a wise man. So, let me end here for now and say, be sure to take good care of yourself and never let anything keep you down when you fall or stumble in life through mistakes, setbacks, or disappointments. Keep rising, be strong, be bold, be confident and courageous. Nothing should or can hold you down unless you permit it to.

Let us recap what we have covered on this discourse on how to make a comeback from mistakes, setbacks, and disappointments in life.

1. Don't live in denial. Acknowledge and come to terms with what has happened.
2. Resist the temptation to start labelling blame (including blaming yourself) for whatever mistake, setback, or disappointment you experience in your life.
3. Don't take things personally
4. Forgive and let go. Don't hold on to grudges.
5. Be active. Don't stay idle.
6. Be patient with yourself and others, but never complacent.
7. Seek and ask for help. Don't suffer in silence.

How ready are you for the change that is coming in your life? Find out in the next chapter.

11

DEALING WITH A DIFFICULT CHANGE IN YOUR LIFE

Whether you like it or not, Change will happen in your life.

Change is destined to happen in your life, many, many times over. The question is, will you be ready to successfully deal with it when it happens?

Brian Tracy, a Canadian-American motivational public speaker and self-development author, once said that "the forces of Change impact everything you do. The rate of change is accelerating week by week and month by month, and the speed and variety of Change is something over which you have no control, and about which you have no choice. The only decision you have to make is whether you are going to be a master of Change or a victim of it. Are you going to be a master of circumstances or a creature of circumstances? It will be one or the other, but the impact of Change will be forced upon you, whatever you do".

I agree with Brian. Change is inevitable, and it is up to you to make the most of it or crash under it.

In this chapter, we are going to look at some ways of making the most of the changes we will experience in life and not crush under them.

You see, change is a constant in life, and you can count on it to happen. Seasons will change, the way you live your life will change, people will change, - perhaps even faster than you can imagine, technology will change. Apart from the following three things: *the principles governing human behaviour, the laws of the natural universe, and God*, everything changes.

Here is the thing, living this life is like travelling in an unpredictable journey. And this journey is made up of mini journeys. One of these mini journeys could be called childhood, another could be adolescence, then we have education, yet another could be marriage, business or entrepreneurship, success, relationships, incarceration, rejection, loneliness etc. They are all series of small journeys in your unpredictable journey of life. Some of them are sprints, and others are marathons. And whatever journey you find yourself in, it will be wrought with ups and downs, one change after another. A moment of triumph here, and a moment of sadness or failure there, this thing, and that thing, here and there. And so on, and so forth.

We all know that change happens, don't we? Why is it then that we often find it difficult to deal with it? Especially the sort of changes that we don't like, the difficult ones. In fact, many people, will fight 'tooth and nail' to keep the status quo and won't want to know anything to do with change of any sort that will tamper with the way of life that they are happy with. They will resist that change at all costs.

The question is, why is that the case? Why do people almost invariably resist change that goes against the way things are?

Well, there could be many reasons for that, but I think it's primarily because of the fear of the unknown, and also because of the desire to stay with the familiar. You see, the unknown is often seen by most people as risky and, therefore, to be avoided, while the familiar is seen as safe, and, as such, to be maintained. There is comfort in the known and familiar. We humans would prefer things for the most part (especially what we perceive as the good things), to remain unchanged forever.

However, the truth of the matter is this; change, whether good or bad, will have its course, and you'll only resist it, if you do, at your own peril. Things do and will change. That we feel stress when they do does not change the fact that change is inevitable, there is no permanent condition in life apart from change – it will always happen.

There is no need fighting or resisting something that is inevitable, the wise thing to do is to find a way to successfully deal with it when it happens in your life.

The question then is this; how do you actually do it and not be overwhelmed, especially if it is a difficult change to handle? How do you manage it?

Well, let me draw your attention to an eight letter word called - **optimism** and the powerful role it can play in helping you deal with change whenever and wherever it happens to you.

The online dictionary defines optimism as "hopefulness and confidence about the future or the success of something".

Being hopeful and confident about the prospects of the change you are facing or are bound to face, is a very powerful antidote to the anxiety and fear sometimes associated with change. Hope gives you something to hold on and look forward to, while confidence gives you the strength for holding on to that hope, and the vision of better things to come.

In my view, it is about being strong and of good courage. That's what **optimism** is all about. Strength comes from being hopeful, but then you need to have the courage to put that strength to work for your benefit.

Change of any sort can be challenging. Change can be slow and gradual, or sudden and fast. However, the most difficult change to handle is one that happens suddenly. Sudden change has very devastating consequences if it is not properly dealt with. This kind of change often stirs up all sorts of emotions and feelings in people, including feelings of extreme anxiety and fear. And for most people, if these anxious and fearful thoughts and feelings are not dealt with swiftly and decisively, they will potentially find themselves travelling the rabbit hole of depression and hopelessness. So, yes, being optimistic amid the changes happening in your life will help you live with a sense of purpose and meaning, and you will be in a better position to deal with the effects of any sort of change much more decisively than if you were pessimistic about it. Optimism gives you that drive and courage you need to navigate the anxious path brought about by change and to do so with grace, dignity, and foresight.

In short, optimism is your secret weapon in the fight against this unrelenting and sometimes sudden thing called Change. Optimism helps you you to be strong and of good courage.

But how can optimism help you overcome the challenges and difficulties orchestrated by change? You may ask.

Well, the **first thing** is to always be ready for anything, especially being psychologically ready. I call it being mentally strong, and that is optimism at work here.

The thing is, change can, and will happen at any time, with or without your permission or knowledge. Change doesn't have to send you an email to notify you that it is on its way. No, it won't. Change sometimes just happens. It can happen when you least expect it to do so, and your life can take a turn for good or bad, all in a moment's notice. So, whether you find yourself in paradise or in "hell", so to say, you need to be able to deal with that situation well, and being mentally strong, will help you.

Mental strength is a key part of optimism, and you should do everything you can to ensure that you are developing, building, or improving your mental strength and health every day.

Secondly, expect things to change in your life. There is no permanent condition in life apart from change, and you need to be okay with change happening, it is normal, and in a way, you should expect it.

I like what Tilman Fertitta said in his book titled 'Shut up and Listen' about expecting change. He said: "By anticipating change, you don't just change with the times – you change the times themselves."

I like that.

Yes, anticipate change, know that at some point, things will change, and in that way, you will not be shocked when that happens. And you will also be more apt to successfully deal with it, than if change happened as a shock to you.

Thirdly, make up your mind to thrive in the change. Promise yourself, no, let me go further and say, assure yourself that, regardless of the nature of the change that is happening or about to happen in your life, you will make the most of it. You will not allow yourself to be brought down or sidestepped, and you will do whatever it takes to thrive in it; doing all you can to take full advantage of the situation you find yourself in, whatever that situation may be.

Fourthly, come to terms with change when it happens, don't fight it but strive to be its master, and not its victim. Many years ago, one of my tutors in the accountancy course I was doing at the time, made a remark that helped inform my approach to change. He said, "*come to terms with your situation, and you will have a breakthrough.*" At the time, I was going through some challenging stuff in my life, and to me, his remark seemed both heartless and difficult to accept or even consider. However, I later realised that it was the right thing I needed to do. Challenging though it was to take his advice, I decided to apply it, and I came to terms with the challenges I was facing at the time. I must say though that, the thought of coming to terms with what I was going through in my life seemed like a stupid and defeatist thing to do. However, in some strange way, it paved the way for a change of fortunes for me. And that was a big lesson for me.

Over the years, I have come to fully appreciate and embrace that remark – "*come to terms with your situation, and you will have a breakthrough*". It is true.

I have, since then, encountered very challenging times in life, very defining moments that I would have otherwise, naturally been inclined to resist and resent, but instead, I accepted them. I came to terms with what was going on as it were, and in doing so, I found myself facing such times with hope, courage, unwavering faith and confidence, and believing that something good would come out of them. And whenever I have persisted and maintained that level of faith and assurance, things indeed turned out to be well for me in the end.

However, coming to terms with the fact that change is happening or is imminent, does not and should not in any way mean being passive and just go with the flow. No. That's not what it means. What it means is preparing yourself for what is on the horizon and doing all you can to stand strong and confident when dealing with those changes. The goal is to find ways to benefit from the Change rather than feel broken, defeated, or disenfranchised by it.

The truth of the matter is this; for most people today, they feel defeated, let down, powerless and even depressed because they have either refused to acknowledge that Change is here, or they have no idea what to do to deal with the changes happening in their lives.

If you are currently going through some sort of change in your life, a change that is upsetting you or draining your mental energy, perhaps it is the loss of a job, or the loss of a loved one, or a business failure, or it could be something to do with your relationships, or maybe it is a false accusation you are dealing with, or perhaps it is an illness. I don't really know what it is you are going through or dealing with right now, but whatever it is, can I first of all say that I understand what you are going through, and I feel your pain. I know what it means to suffer loss and how difficult it is to deal with the pain of loss. I know how it feels when you are falsely accused, and I understand the loneliness of feeling rejected, I know how tough it can be to feel alone. I have been there before, and it's not a place I ever want to return to if I were to always have my way in life.

Now, if you are going through any sort of tough time right now, due to some form of change that has happened in your life, I recommend first of all that you come to terms with the fact that what has happened, has happened or is happening, and don't try to deny it. Don't 'bury your head in the sand', or try to protest, or cry out in disbelief saying no, no, no, this is not, or can't be happening to me. Well, that wouldn't be wise. Denying it won't accomplish anything, or make it go away. In fact, it may make things even worse. So, come to terms with it, acknowledge it and then ask yourself what you can do right now, to move on with your life and find peace and meaning in the midst of the change that you are in. And whatever insights you receive, make sure you act on them.

History archives give us a record of individuals who in the face of very challenging circumstances in their lives stayed optimistic and steadfast and were able to rise above those challenges and come out better off in the end. They fought the good fight, being strong and of good courage.

Mahatma Ghandi and Nelson Mandela are perhaps some notable examples of triumph over adversity in the way they demonstrated so pragmatically the power of optimism over Change. I will in this discourse, take the example of Mr Mandela and explore it a bit further.

Nelson Mandela was an activist against apartheid in South Africa. His fight against the system that was perpetuating injustice in his country led him to be jailed for 27 years, 18 of which were spent in solitary confinement in Robben Island.

During his time in prison, Mandela suffered the loss of his mother and his son, and he was not permitted to attend their funerals. He suffered a few ailments along the way too, but despite all these adversities, he kept bouncing back from despair and hopelessness. And after that great ordeal, Mandela went on later to become the first black president of the Republic of South Africa.

That was quite a remarkable journey and turnaround, wouldn't you agree? From a prisoner to head of state. That is quite something. It reminds me of the story of Joseph, written in the book of Genesis in the Bible, and how he also rose from being a prisoner to the second in command in Egypt, many many centuries ago.

Anyway, how did he do it? How come Mandela did not lose his mind and become resentful bitter or even insane. What was his secret? In fact, it is widely reported that Nelson Mandela emerged with an even stronger spirit after his isolation in Robben Island and later in Cape Town. He proved not only to survive his banishment for 27 years but also thrived in it. Twenty-seven years is a long time for anyone to go through the kind of ordeal Mr Mandela went through and still come out unbroken and in good mental health. It is quite remarkable!

Think about it; going through such pain, isolation, abuse, discouragement, and many other unspeakable things, and refuse to be defeated but rather emerge victoriously transformed, is truly a remarkable achievement, and I am confident that his optimism for a better South Africa, combined with his strong will and good courage, as well as his decision to forgive those who imprisoned him, are factors that played a significant part in his victorious transformation from a prisoner to head of state.

It was by having a cause bigger than himself - the liberation of others from apartheid, that prevented him wallowing in self-pity for almost three decades. I believe he still had hope that, that liberation would happen. Mandela in a way became a master of the prison imposed upon him and was able to appear dignified in the face of it, and I believe his optimistic state of mind contributed a lot to his survival. It was like the rays of the light of hope and confidence shining into the darkness of despair and hopelessness.

We can learn a lot from Nelson Mandela, can we not?

We can learn that in the face of the defining moments of our lives, those tough and challenging moments that sometimes don't make sense at all at the time, we can decide to believe against all the odds, and summon all of our strength and courage, and say to ourselves that we can make it, that it will be okay in the end.

We can also learn the value of forgiveness in keeping bitterness and resentment at bay, and thus help maintain good mental strength and health.

When times are tough, we must look to the future with optimism. We must be optimistic about what the future holds for us personally as individuals, and collectively as a community or nation, and not give in to fear and despair. We have to rise and keep rising, no matter how many times we fall. Staying down is not an option. Up we rise, forward we match - clearheaded and resolute.

You must not give room or give way to cynicism, self-pity, and discouragement, and you must not give in to pressure. You must rather stand firm, steadfast and stay focussed and calm. Ignore the naysayers, stay positive, believe in the inherent blessing in every adversity, and stay relentlessly optimistic. Step into the realm of optimism – the realm of faith and confidence, the realm of strength and good courage. You have to get there, that is your safety zone. For you see, there is some inherent good that often comes wrapped up in the seemingly disastrous circumstances of our lives, and optimism will help you find it and it will also help you make sense of it all. How? I don't know how, but I know it does.

A lot of changes will happen in your life many, many times over. That is not a prophecy. It is merely stating the obvious, and you must choose how you will deal with those changes.

One way is to be cynical and pessimistic, and the other way is to be realistic and optimistic. Those two choices are mutually exclusive, and you must decide which one you will embrace each time you find yourself dealing with Change or facing the defining moments of your life- the precursors for change.

My hope is that you will choose to be relentlessly optimistic and steadfastly strong and courageous, no matter the sort of change you will encounter in your life.

Believe a better outcome is possible in all circumstances and keep that belief alive. Don't be frightened or intimidated by Change. Change gives every one of us the opportunity to improve our lives in some way or area and thereby to reinvent ourselves so to say, and it also gives us the opportunity to correct past mistakes and see things in a new light.

When going through a difficult change in your life, surround yourself with positive, and optimistic people, read edifying books, do those things that bring you strength, joy, and meaning. Be kind to yourself, forgive those whom you believe have caused you harm or caused the unpleasant change you now have to deal with, and don't lose hope for a better and brighter future. I hope you'll do so.

Let me end here by briefly recapitulating what I have presented to you in this discourse. Here are four things you need to bear in mind and act upon if you are to successfully deal with change in your life whenever, and wherever it happens to you, and regardless of its nature – whether it is a good or difficult change:

1. Develop or build your mental strength daily to help you cope with change as, and when it happens.
2. Be okay with change happening, in fact, expect it to happen. There is no permanent condition in life apart from change.
3. Make up your mind to thrive in change and not be overwhelmed by it. Be its master and not its victim.

4. Come to terms with change when it happens, don't fight it but acknowledge it, and look for opportunities in it.

Be an optimist! Fight the good fight of faith.

> *The truth of the matter is this; Change, whether good or bad, will have its course, and you'll only resist it, if you do, at your own peril. The wise thing to do is to find a way to successfully deal with it when it happens in your life, and not try to resist it.*

12

ONE THING THAT RICH PEOPLE DO THAT POOR PEOPLE DON'T

The people you choose and keep company with, is no joking matter

Is it possible that you might be struggling in life because you are trying to do everything on your own, without a mentor or advisor for guidance? Rich people don't generally do that. They have mentors and advisors.

Have you considered getting a **Mentor**?

Mentoring is when one individual actively and willingly passes their knowledge and wisdom onto another person. It is one of the oldest forms of influence and knowledge sharing. It is a relationship between two people with the goal of professional and personal development. The "mentor" is usually an experienced individual who shares knowledge, experience, and advice with a less experienced person, or "mentee."

Pursuing your dreams can often be a lonely journey, and that's why it is imperative that you enlist the help and guidance of a mentor. Rich and successful people do this all the time. They understand the value of counsel.

A mentor is more like someone you are willing to be accountable to. They should be somebody you respect and for whom you value their opinion and suggestions. I believe that having a good mentor is an invaluable and indispensable part of success in life.

With that in mind, here are three things you can do to help you find a mentor for yourself.

i. Identify what you would like to do or accomplish

What is it that you ultimately desire to have? What do you want to succeed at? You need to be clear about it. Clarity is the first building block for success in life.

ii. Select your mentor

Once you've identified what you would like to do, or to accomplish in life, you should then think about someone who is exceptionally experienced or talented in that area, industry or profession, and has a good reputation. It could be someone you know personally, or it could be a leader in your profession or perhaps someone who is recognised as a top authority in the area you want to specialise in.

Whoever they are, be sure to do your research to verify that they have a proven track record and that they are truly successful. Get at least ten of them – i.e. a list of ten potential mentors. Once you have done so, you should then,

iii. Create a strategic plan to contact them

Here, the most important thing is to be sincere and straight to the point because that generally goes a long way to helping you get what you want in life. So, you could say something like this to your potential mentor(s):

"Hello, Mr/Ms (name). My name is Frank. We haven't met yet, and I know you are a busy person, so I'll be brief. I am ... (mention what your profession is, your field of study or anything that clearly describes your vocation at this present time).

Looking at your career and achievements over the years, I think you have done a fantastic job, building your (professional credentials or business empire or whatever it is they have accomplished). I am sure you had some real challenges when you were first starting out, and it is really admirable to see what you have achieved.

Well, I am still in those early stages, trying to figure everything out how to eventually become as successful as you are.

The reason I am writing/giving you a call, Mr/Ms (Name), is to ask whether you would kindly consider being my mentor. All that would mean is spending 10 minutes on the phone with me once a week and 30 minutes face to face meeting

once every month, so I could ask you a few questions and learn from you and your success.

When making the first contact with your researched mentor to be, get right to the point. Busy people (of which your proposed mentor is more likely to be) appreciate this. Don't socialise. Stick to a well-prepared script using a conversational tone. For example, at the end of your letter or call, say something like: *"Would you be open to that? I would really appreciate it so much."*

It is vital that you control the conversation in the initial contact. Say what you want to say, ask the closing question, and then shut up.

When you ask that closing question – *"Would you be open to that?"* the answer will usually be "Yes" or "No". If it's "Yes", control your excitement and ask a follow-up question - *"When would be a good time to call you in the next few weeks?"*

Confirm the specific time for your first call or meeting and send a thank you note to them right away.

If it's a "No", well, contact the next person in your list of potential mentors you researched until one of them says "Yes". If the first lot of ten say "NO" to you, get a fresh list of 10 more potential mentors and carry on calling or writing to them. You have to persist. One of them will eventually say "Yes" to you. Don't give up.

Remember, before you make the first call, it's useful to have at hand as much information as possible from your research about your potential mentor as far as his professional achievements are concerned and any projects he or she has done, or is currently involved with.

Like I said before, having a mentor is essential to success in life and I hope you will do your best to get yourself one.

Advisors

Most rich and successful people I know have advisors with whom they take counsel and discuss sticky problems.

However, advisors must be selected with much care. They should be people of integrity, people who have good judgement, wide experience, diverse talents, and expertise in areas in which you may be weak, and they should be above all, people who you can get on well with in a spirit of harmony.

Consider your advisors' advice but make your own decisions. Ultimately, the buck always stops with you. Only you know what is right for you, and you will have to make your decisions fully aware that you will live with the impact and consequences of those decisions.

Attention

The other thing rich and successful people know how to do very well is to get and hold the attention of vast amounts of people.

What you need to understand about attention is that attention is a leverage point, and he who holds and controls the attention of others has enormous power. And if you know anything about power, you know that power helps you create wealth.

The so-called social media influencers for example, are people who have mastered the art of grabbing and holding the attention of other people and using that attention as leverage with companies and businesses that want to market their products or services to the influencer's audience. The marketing agreements struck often result in the influencer being handsomely rewarded with big bucks.

Rich and successful people understand the power of attention and they use it to their advantage. For they know that where attention goes, power flows. And where power flows, money is present, either to be given, or to be taken. And so, they are quite careful about who, where, or what they give their attention to, and they do so, intentionally, and intelligently. Poor and unsuccessful people on the other hand have not yet mastered the proper use of their attention, and they indiscriminately direct it according to their feelings, and more to unprofitable ends, like binge watching TV, for example.

Now, allow me for a moment if you will, to take up the role of being your unofficially appointed mentor and advisor to say these few remarks to you:

Make sure you are good with money. You must manage your money well. Don't waste or misuse it. You see, not many people, worldwide, know how to manage their money well, and it is no surprise that many people's finances are is dismal states. I know, because I used to be one of them, but not anymore. And you don't have to be one of them either. Choose to manage your money well. I have already talked about money in the chapter called 'Why You Don't have Enough Money and What You Can do About It. Check it out if you need to read it again.

Here is another thing you need to manage well too - your physical and mental health. Very important. Do not neglect to look after your body and mental wellbeing. I talked about this in-depth earlier in the chapter about 'Small Changes That Can Make a Huge Difference in Your Life' and you can refer to it from the table of contents.

And doubtless, as discussed in-depth on the chapter about relationships; you need to manage your relationships very well too.

Be an independent thinker and don't let other people do your thinking for you. In other words, have your own mind, and make your own decisions, and be willing to take responsibility for your decisions and actions!

Here is a principle that has enormously helped me in life, and I hope you can adopt it too. Jesus Christ said it and it is this; ***do to others, what you would have them do to you*** – The golden rule of life.

Be true to yourself and never pretend to be who you are not, or to be somebody else. Be authentically you. Pretence and false appearances will lead you nowhere but to failure and misery. Avoid that path and stay true to who you are and grow to become a better version of yourself.

Here is something else worth remembering; The What you privately speak about to yourself will prevail. So, learn to faithfully speak the Words of power, and words of wisdom over yourself, your life, your family, your business and finances, and the world you live in. Hold fast to those words in faith, never wavering. Soon or later, you will start embodying what you privately declare to yourself and about yourself.

In life, once you have chosen to do something, take it to the next level by overdelivering on what you have chosen to do. Go the extra mile. Do more than you are asked or expected to do. Do it every time and do it willingly. Go the extra mile and adopt a performance frame of mind. When you are in a performance frame of mind, you will choose to carefully plan and programme yourself for the performance as opposed to when you are in a frame of mind of 'just doing something'. The difference in outcome is huge. I know so. For you see, Performance requires skill, attention, and planning.

Next,

A wise man once said: 'Don't tell people what to do (not many people like to be told what to do), instead, show them what is possible and let them choose whatever the heck they want to do.'

And whenever you have to deal with a challenging or difficult situation in your life, be strong and courageous and do not flinch in the face of challenges or difficulties. Be open to new possibilities and to better ways of doing things.

Risk is not knowing or understanding what you are doing. Put another way, doing what you don't know or understand is risky. So, make risk management one of your top priorities in life. Ensure that you are thoroughly well acquainted with the things and people you get involved with, in life. And, when dealing with things in life, distinguish which ones to deal with based on fact and which ones to deal with based on faith and when to use both. Buying a car, for example, is dealt with on the basis of facts, understanding the existence of God is on the basis of faith, but starting and running a business is dealt with on the basis of both facts and faith but mostly faith.

Your conscience depends on your basic beliefs concerning right or wrong. And so, if your basic beliefs are true, realistic, and sensible, your conscience becomes a true ally, friend, and guide in dealing with the real world and sailing upon the ethical sea. It nudges you to' think twice' when you contemplate doing something wrong. It warns you of danger that could be done to you or others, and you will do well to take heed to what this type of conscience tells you. However, if your basic beliefs are themselves wrong and untrue, unrealistic, or not sensible, it stands to say that your conscience will indeed be warped and obeying such a conscience will lead to misery and not happiness, both for you and those around you. Therefore, if you are to let your conscience be your guide, it must be based on truth. Otherwise blindly obeying your conscience can be a recipe for disaster. The more developed your mind is, the better your conscience will serve you. I, therefore, recommend that you keep renewing your mind; study life, understand things that work for you and those that don't, embrace change positively and study the Bible.

Moving on, if you don't want to be deceived by tricksters and people who want to take advantage of you, think accurately, and insist on having the facts and evidence of everything presented to you because almost everything, can be proved and verified. So, be careful when people tell you to just believe what they say without evidence. Rather be like a scientist or detective who insists on having facts and evidence before giving credence to anything.

One other thing I would like to bring to your attention is the importance of doing or saying things at the right time and the need to embrace patience. There is nothing in life that has the immediate effect of curtailing your progress or success like poor timing. When you have to, it is not enough to just say or do the right thing, no, it is also essential that you say or do it at the right time. You have to be patient and wait for the right moment. "There is a time for everything, and a season for every activity under the heavens", so it says in Ecclesiastes 3:1.

Timing is critical in our discourses in life. And the essential requirement for keeping the right timing is patience and discernment.

And as important as mastering the timing for doing things is, one other thing I would recommend you do is to do your best to look good, not because you want to impress other people, but, because people initially judge you by appearances. Appearances, in the end, will not matter if you can't perform your allotted task as required, but they sure do give you a good head start. Besides, looking good affects you psychologically in a positive way. So, take care to look good, dress smart and be well-groomed.

You need the strict self-discipline and determination to make sure that your sovereign power of choice is put to good use and followed up with. And never take anything in your life for granted.

Don't be afraid to have critics, they will always be there no matter what you do. And the more you advance in life, the fiercer your critics will be. Relax, that's just the way of life. And don't be overly concerned about pleasing everyone either. I say so because it is very difficult, or nearly impossible to always please everybody, however much you try. So, don't lose sleep over those who won't be pleased by your best efforts.

Live your life the best way you can and don't limit yourself, or let yourself down, and if you do (let yourself down), bounce right up, learn from it, and move on. Make the most of what you have and strive to make yourself better every day. Be accountable and take 100% responsibility for what you want to see happen in your life.

Finally, ...

In this life, people will judge you. You will be judged by your looks, and appearance - how you dress and all that, you will be judged by your accent, you will be judged by the size of your bank account - how much money you've got, you will be judged by the colour of your skin, and you will be judged by what you believe - the faith you profess (your religion) etc. The bottom line is that you will be judged. However, the greatest judgement, and the one that really matters is your own judgement of yourself, your own view of yourself. How do you view yourself and your life? That's the critical question and I hope you view yourself and life favourably, otherwise, what hope have you got? And did you know that how you view yourself will even bias how you think God views you? So, I hope you can see why it is critical that you view or judge yourself favourably.

Be authentically true to yourself and pay no attention to the critics and naysayers. Don't take things personally, and instead of assuming things and creating all sorts of stories and befuddlements, seek clarity about things, and ALWAYS do your best in everything you decide to do.

If you do the above, you will be right on your way to great and amazing things.

Thanks for listening.

Let us consider how to deal with emotional pain, next.

13

WHAT TO DO WHEN YOU FEEL HURT AND EMOTIONALLY OVERWHELMED

Nothing in our lives comes to stay. Everything is temporal, good, or bad. Take courage, even this (whatever it is) will pass.

Often, the challenges we face in life can be so overwhelming that we find ourselves travelling the rabbit hole of depression and utter helplessness.

Sometimes, we inadvertently bring these challenges upon ourselves, and at other times we believe others are to blame for our troubles, and as such, we get so mad at them. In fact, sometimes, we get so worked up that we are prepared to strike back at those we believe are the cause of our emotional pain and broken hearts. Or we may vow to get even with them at some point in the future if we don't have the capacity to strike back now.

However, the bible has a different approach. It states: "*If someone has done you wrong, do not repay him with a wrong. Try to do what everyone considers to be good. Do everything possible on your part to live in peace with everybody. Never take revenge, my friends, but instead let God's anger do it. For the scripture says, 'I will take revenge, I will pay back, says the Lord.' Instead, as the scripture says: 'If your enemies are hungry, feed them; if they are thirsty, give them a drink; for by doing this you will make them burn with shame.' Do not let evil defeat you; instead, conquer evil with good."* **Romans 12:17-21**

I like to say it this way - *two wrongs can never make a right, and a tit for tat attitude creates more problems than it solves. Seek peace.*

The truth is, emotional pain, as you may well know, is real and often hard to deal with. What I want to do in this chapter is share with you an experience that was quite emotionally challenging for me, and how I dealt with it, and I am hoping that it might resonate with someone out there who might be going through some emotionally challenging situation in their life right now.

Late in my twenties, I was involved in a romantic relationship, and that relationship left me very heartbroken. I felt betrayed and lied to, I felt taken for a ride, and I was very, very upset and disappointed. All sorts of things were going on in my mind at the time. I was angry with myself for getting into such a mess, and worst of all, I felt helpless. It was really tough for me.
I subsequently became withdrawn for a while. I felt lost.

That went on for a couple of months, and then one day, I decided to gather the courage to talk to the lady concerned about what she had done to me, and how it had devastated me. I 'poured' out my heart and openly talked about the hurt I was feeling, and how I felt taken for a ride, and let down by her.

Tears trickled down my cheeks as I spoke and unburdened himself. I was uploading all my bottled-up feelings and emotions, releasing them as it were.

She was kind enough to just sit there and listen to me.

After a while, and what seemed like my last word on the matter, I breathed a big deep sigh of relief, and you could see that I looked calmer and more relaxed. A gentle smile started to form on my face.

I don't know what happened, but I felt lighter, and I think what helped was that she just listened without interrupting, or arguing with me.

I look back now, and I think that was the moment when I had closure with her, and I was able to move on with my life.

You see, my story is not unique, many of us carry with us burdens, disappointments, betrayals, rejections, and all manner of things that are weighing us down and 'choking' the life out of us.

The thing is, having bottled up negative emotions can only serve to do you harm and not good. The best thing you can do for yourself is to release those negative feelings and emotions, otherwise, they will keep you bound in a precarious psychological state.

One of the best ways to release bottled up negative emotions is to talk to somebody about what you are going through or experiencing. In my case, it was the same person whom I had a problem with. It might not be the case with you, but regardless, you will still need to find somebody to talk to about what you are going through.

Understandably, it might be hard to do so, but you have to gather the courage to do it - talk to somebody.

Now, talking to somebody does not mean just anybody. There are two categories of people you can speak to in this instance. They should either be part of the problem, or part of the solution.

Let me explain,

Say, for example, you feel betrayed by a colleague, and as a result, you start feeling resentment, anger, and hatred towards them. What do you think you should do when that happens?

Well, you need to get whatever is causing the feelings of anger and resentment sorted. Your first point of call would be to talk it over with your colleague and let them know how you feel about them betraying your confidence or trust or whatever it is they have done. Communicate your feelings and concerns to them with a view to seeking understanding and reconciliation.

If it is hard for you to do that, then consider talking to somebody whom you know can listen to both of you without prejudice (your manager, pastor, or mentor perhaps).

Do not, however, just go and 'pour out' your heart to any ear. That might actually be counterproductive and even cause you more emotional turmoil. Not everyone is empathetic enough or has the patience to deal with the emotional challenges you might be facing.

Now, sometimes, the emotional rollercoasters you go through might have nothing to do with what anybody has done to you, but it might be because of the general state of affairs in your family, community or country.

Genuine, legitimate concerns like for example frustration due to lack of employment, frustration with taking long to get the right marriage partner, frustration for loss of a loved one, or for mistakes you have made in the past that are now causing you lots of trouble, it could be anything, really, who knows. All these things can pause very serious emotional challenges for many people. Any normal person would feel emotionally overwhelmed should they have to deal with them.

However, being proactive and not allowing these legitimate concerns to build up emotional banks that will reach dangerous levels, is a wise thing to do.

If you allow yourself to be emotionally overwhelmed, you might end up being like a 'walking time bomb waiting to explode' (excuse my military language) and anyone who crosses you in the slightest, risks being on the onslaught of your unsolicited emotional outburst.

The wise thing to do is to empty yourself of those frustrations as often as you can and as soon as possible.

You have to nip problems in the bud before they grow into more serious and harder to deal with issues.

Dealing with trouble promptly, is usually the best approach and is generally more cost-effective financially, relationally, and emotionally, than hoping that the trouble will go away on its own accord.

Just remember that nobody is immune to challenges. We all have our own fair share of challenges to deal with, and from time to time, we will need a shoulder to lean on.

No man is an Island, we need each other, and we should be there for each other, in good times as well as in challenging ones too.

The secret to resolving the challenges we encounter in life and to be at peace with ourselves and others is to accentuate the solution(s) more than the problems at hand.

So, I wonder, do you feel overwhelmed with life's challenges right now? Do you feel hurt? Do you feel lonely and helpless? Do you feel emotionally weighed down? If so, I urge you to take action, talk it over with somebody you can trust to listen to you without prejudice or judgement.

By talking things over, you will feel relieved, and you will find insight and inspiration to move on, or to start all over. The lights will be turned on, and the darkness dispelled. Solutions to your predicament will also somehow start emerging.

However, what if you can't get yourself to talk to somebody, how can you rescue yourself from bad thoughts and negative emotions? How can you help yourself when you find yourself constantly thinking negatively?

Well, by the time you find yourself deeply engrossed in negative thinking, it is not much help trying to replace the negative thoughts with positive ones, at least not at that very moment.

The most effective way to combat bad and negative thoughts is positive action, i.e. get up and do something positive for yourself, or somebody else, like: giving charity, volunteering, going for a workout in the gym, helping somebody in need, singing and dancing to your favourite song, start giving thanks for the things you have, etc. Just do something positive. That's how you drive negative thoughts and emotions out. And once you have driven them out, contemplate on the positive action(s) you just did, and read and meditate on some positive affirmations.

Trying to get yourself to start thinking positive when you are overwhelmed with negative emotions is very challenging unless you do as I have suggested in the preceding paragraph.

Here are other things you can do as well

Sometime ago, I paused this question to the members of the social media groups I belong to on Facebook, here is the question: "*What do you normally do when you are down, feeling really low but want to get out of that slump?*

There were over 230 comments posted in response to that question, but I have just picked a few for you here:

Michael Said: "*Take the good with the bad, meaning I think of everything else that is good that has happened to me and what I am learning and sacrificing*".

Elisa said: "*I almost had a meltdown two days ago over a task that seemed very difficult. I let my feelings run their course, then put on some music, danced a little and went back to the task I needed to complete. It worked pretty well. I was able to focus and finish that pending, seemingly insurmountable task*".

Michelle said: "*I journal. Read a book. Watch a movie. Reach out to someone. Watch something positive and uplifting on YouTube like Tony. Write a Gratitude Log. Write an action scene for my YA fantasy novel...*"

Mich said: "*Right now, one of the things that works for me to feel centered is listening to spiritual talks... and aromatherapy...*"

Rich Said:
"*3 different things i do*
Good question though. If I'm deeply depressed
1) Inspirational movies, Music , passive things

2) just bumm out
I get up clean organize my car, room, house, garage.
Makes feel better. Go for walk , visit fun friends
3) just down for the day

I get up , dress up , never give up. Read , visit inspiring friends. Do something uncomfortable share my life serve people Basically hey out of myself."

Pauletta said: "*Go for a walk in nature or dance to music Peace be with you.*"

Ali said: "*I put on some music that makes me want to dance like no one is watching. Or I will write down a list of everything I'm grateful for. But most of all, and it's not for everyone, i go do some volunteer work at a homeless shelter or woman's refuge and remind myself of how fortunate I am compared to others and get out of 'victim' mode.*"

Kath said: "*Currently - Listen to Jason Mraz https://m.youtube.com/watch?v=BFkTu8Y1KLs*"

Laura said: "*Music ,sing ,dance , it changes your mindset.*"

Ken said: "*Remember You have a Purpose in Life, being rock bottom means there's only way now & that is UP.*
Look in the mirror n repeat an affirmation ' I love n Approve of Myself'. Do 15 mins of fast exercise."

Betina said: "*I pray for other people in similar situations and I thank God for being still well.*"

Katherine said: "*Volunteer your time to serve others.. in turn you serve and better yourself. Trust me this is the key!*

Plus of course, eating well, exercising, yoga, meditation and reading books that open your mind and encourage you to do more... demand more of yourself!"

Ashleen said: "*Fake laugh until you're really laughing..lol is hilarious.*"

Nicky said: "*I crank up my favourite tunes kick off my shoes and dance around the room like no one's watching. Try it you'll love it.*"

I hope that what some of these kind people wrote in reply can be of help to you.

Finally, do these four things on a daily basis:

i. *Be authentically true to yourself, don't lie to yourself.*
ii. *Train yourself not to take things personally. There is a lot going on in the world and everybody is dealing with their own issues in life. Stuff just happens as people try to sort out their own issues and in the process you might be affected, just remember that when that happens, it is not personal.*
iii. *Don't make assumptions. Seek clarification whenever you are not sure of something instead of making assumptions that may be totally wrong and emotionally challenging.*
iv. *Always do the best you can, where you are, with what you have. Don't stress yourself out trying to be perfect.*

I hope you found this chapter useful. Fittingly, let's move on and talk about happiness, next.

14

HOW AND WHERE TO FIND HAPPINESS

Why you are sometimes not happy and what to do about it.

The late Dr John A. Schindler - a medical Doctor and author of How to Live 365 Days a Year once defined happiness as "*A state of the mind in which our thinking is pleasant most of the time*".

Maxwell Maltz, in his book; Psycho cybernetics, said of happiness that; "*Happiness is native to the human mind and its physical machine. We think better, perform better, feel better, and are healthier when we are happy. Even our physical sense organs work better*".

Psychosomatic medicine has proved that our stomachs, liver, heart, and all our internal organs function better when we are happy.

Thousands of years ago, wise King Solomon said in his Proverbs: "*A cheerful heart is good medicine, but a crushed spirit dries up the bones.*". Proverbs 17:22

Harvard psychologists studied the correlation between happiness and criminality and concluded that the old Dutch proverb, '*Happy people are never wicked*,' was scientifically true. They found that a majority of criminals came from unhappy homes and had a history of unhappy human relationships.

Generally, by and large, whether in business, social circles or in any endeavour in life, optimistic, cheerful people who looked on the bright side of things were more successful than pessimistic people.

Now, with news about the challenges to the world economy, wars, chronic illnesses, gun and knife crime, poverty, hunger, soaring personal debts, broken marriages etc., is there any room for happiness in the world today? Especially for anyone facing any of the aforementioned challenges.

Happiness, it seems has done a runner, or has it?

In this chapter, we are going to look at happiness, and attempt to answer this question – who is responsible for your happiness? And what will it take for you to experience happiness regularly?

The truth is, when it is all said and done, when everything is done and dusted, ultimately, your HAPPINESS is determined by one person and one person alone - YOU. Your happiness is personal, you are the one responsible for it.

Those words set the tone for what the rest of this chapter reveals.
It appears that in our popular thinking about happiness, we have managed to get the cart before the horse. 'Be kind and loving to other people, and you will be happy' We say, or, I would be happy, we say to ourselves, if I were successful and healthy, or if I had this thing, or that thing, etc.

It might be nearer the truth if we said, 'Be happy - and you will be good, more successful, healthier, feel and act more charitably towards others.'

In life, you need to train yourself to arrive at a point where you are okay being you and not being concerned about offending anyone for being you.

You should arrive to a point in your life where you stop trying to get people to like you, and simply just be yourself. People can take it or leave it, that's what's on offer, and it's the only choice. And it's not that you will offer that choice in a braggadocious way, no, not at all, but rather in a gentle, and assertive way, and no hard feelings meant.

The thing is, very few people are this way. Most are trying to figure out how to get others to approve of them or like them. However, that's not a good strategy because the more you NEED others to like you, the less likely they are to do so, and then inevitably, you'll start developing feelings of unworthiness and self-pity, that is, if you do not have a strong self-image.

You know what? Never appear NEEDY for anything. Seriously, that's bad, don't do it.

Most needy people I have met are a miserable lot. I say so because I was once in that lot, and I know exactly what I am talking about.

"*The attitude of unhappiness is not only painful, but it is also mean and ugly*," said the late William James - an American philosopher and psychologist, and the first educator to offer a psychology course in the United States.

'*Most people are about as happy as they make up their minds to be*,' said Abraham Lincoln, the 16th president of the United States.

Let us, for a little while, think about what mr Lincoln said, shall we? "*as happy as they make up their minds to be*". What does that even mean? How does it happen? How do you make up your mind to be happy? Hmmm.... (pondering). Interesting question, right?

Well, let's see. Think of a time you saw somebody really happy, can you remember why they were happy?

When I think about it, it's mostly when they have achieved something, or conquered a challenging situation. They might have gotten a job, or a promotion, or won a game, or quiz, or championship etc. In each case, it was about something they were looking forward to attaining and really worked hard at it.

So, thinking about what Abraham Lincoln said– *"..as happy as they make up their minds to be"*, I think one can make up their mind to be happy by deciding to pursue what they like, set a goal about it, and get to work to achieve it. And as for long as they are making strides to achieve that goal and making little wins along the way as they advance to their goal, they will feel happy. Most unhappy people have no goals and are just wondering about in life. Don't be one of them.

Set your own goals, have a burning desire that you are working towards, be optimistic, and have a positive attitude in life.

Psychologist Dr Matthew N. Chappel, said, "*Happiness is purely internal, it is produced, not by objects, but by ideas, thoughts and attitudes which can be developed by the individuals own activities, irrespective of the environment.*"

That is an interesting statement, right? And so, it seems to me that you shouldn't allow yourself to be pushed around, either by people or circumstances. Your happiness is not something that happens to you. It is something that you yourself determine upon, by knowing what you want, setting a goal to attain it, and getting to work to achieve it.

If you wait for happiness to catch up with you or 'just happen' or to be brought to you by others or circumstances, well, you are likely to wait for a very, very long time, my dear.

No one can determine or decide what you will think, or want, but you, yourself. If you wait for circumstances to 'justify' your thinking pleasant thoughts, you are most likely to wait for eternity.

Every day comes with a mixed package of good and evil. No day is at all 100% 'good' or 100% 'bad.' You will find that there are things and 'facts' present in the world and in your personal life at any one time, which will 'justify either a pessimistic and grumpy outlook, or an optimistic and happy outlook. It all depends on what you chose to focus on. It's not a matter of being intellectually honest or dishonest either, good is as real as bad. It all depends on what you are giving your primary attention to, as you move towards achieving your goals.

Remember, you are RESPONSIBLE for your own HAPPINESS, no one else is. Not your government, not your company, not your wife, not your husband, not your pastor, not your children, but you, YOURSELF! Are responsible.

Get creative about the next chapter of your life. Imagine yourself being or possessing those things you so much desire and arouse a sense of happiness within you as you imagine having or possessing those things you so much desire.

If there are problems in your life, focus your mind and thoughts on finding solutions, and not moaning about the problems. Smile, even if everything seems to be going against your wishes and desires. Keep positive, don't give in to despair. The bad will not last forever, stay hopeful, and be busy working on your goals.

Stress is more often linked to focusing your energy and thoughts on problems and not the solutions to the problems you are facing in life. If you put all of your energy and attention into the problem(s) you face, you will have no energy left for the solutions. A helpful thing to do would be to acknowledge the problem and move on to finding a solution to it whilst focusing on more positive things in your life.

You can choose to be the happiest person in the world right now by virtue of the thoughts you choose to dwell upon. I can understand that not everything might be perfect in your life right now, but you can still find reason in your life to cheer up and look on the bright side of things, and with that, transform your internal world and thus your outer world with the radiant glow of hope and joy - happiness.

When for example you look at your bank statement or your finances, and you immediately begin to feel bad and agitated because things are not going according to plan or adding up, or when the perceived reality of your situation begins ruining your day, and start feeling frustrated, fearful and worried, do something right away to change your mental state. Change location, get up and dance, or take a walk or jog or call someone you respect and talk with them. Anything to take your mind dwelling on those issues negatively will help, you can then come back later and look at your situation with a calm rational mind and seek ways to resolve it. Always try to rise above any miserly situations you find yourself in.

That's right, rise above them, and setting goals is one of the ways you can do that.

Having goals that you are actively working towards is important for your state of happiness. So, get busy setting goals for yourself, and working on them. And once you achieve one goal, get on with another one, and another one, like that, and keep moving forward. You'll be surprised how much happiness you will encounter along the way as you set and achieve your goals.

The thing is, you have an inherent goal seeking mechanism within you, and you will be unhappy without goals you truly believe in, and are commited to achieving. And that's why I also believe that it is challenging, or nearly impossible for you to make other people truly happy.

This is because you can't live their life for them and achieve their goals on their behalf, they have to do it themselves for them to experience their own happiness. You can facilitate their being happy like for example helping them with resources for achieving their goals, but overall, happiness is self determined, not others determined.

I think you will really struggle to find happiness and fulfilment in life if you don't have goals you are pursuing. Try to find five to ten people who are really miserable and unhappy and ask them what their goals in life are, chances are that you will get either a blank stare, or a confused look on their faces, meaning, they have no goals, not a clue what they exactly want to do with their lives.

Here is the other thing, happiness will also elude you if you are not whole, that is, if you are not being authentically true to yourself and living your life the best way you can, but rather trying to be someone else or living your life trying to please others in order to fit in or be accepted by them. If you want to be happy, don't do that.

What you can do instead is - maintain a sense of personal integrity, do your best at all times, and be at peace with yourself.

Being at peace with yourself is very, very critical to your sense of happiness and wellbeing, and sort of emanates from the other two – having a sense of personal integrity, and always doing your best. So, do all you can to maintain personal authenticity and loving acceptance of yourself while doing your best, no matter what. Even if that means loosing money, friendships, or whatever else the world calls dear. Never, ever, go against yourself if you want to be happy in life. Be authentically true to yourself, and pursue meaningful goals for yourself, and not goals that will leave you empty and dry because you are trying to seek approval or acceptance from other people.

When it is all said and done, **being happy is a choice and a choice only you can make for yourself**.

> *The truth is, when it is all said and done, when everything is done and dusted, ultimately, your HAPPINESS is determined by one person and one person alone - YOU. Your happiness is personal, you are the one responsible for it.*

15

THE ART OF ASKING AND GETTING WHAT YOU WANT IN LIFE

You can have whatever you want in life if you know how to ask for it.

What do you really want in your life? And why don't you have it already?

Could it be possible that you are stuck in life because you ask not, and even if you ask, could it be that you don't receive what you ask for because you ask amiss? Perhaps you are asking the wrong questions, or the wrong people?

In the next couple of minutes, I will be exploring the ancient art of asking, and I hope that it will give you the impetus to venture further afield to find solutions to some of the predicaments you might be facing in your life right now.

The truth is, we all get by in life by asking, and it doesn't matter what your position or status in life is, asking is part and parcel of our human interconnectedness and interdependence, and it will always be so. We really can't get away from it.

And asking, is of two forms: internal and external.

You ask internally of yourself, a sort of self-reflective questioning, an introspection if you may.

Introspection is a characteristic of a growth mindset, a mindset that is essential for living a well-balanced and productive life.

Each of us needs to make time every so often to ask ourselves questions; questions about our day, questions about what we believe, why we believe what we believe, questions about how we can be better versions of ourselves, questions about what we can do or what we are capable of, etc. These questions are very important in that they help us to see things differently and not be encased in useless rituals, traditions, and superstitions that more often than not, imprison us.

It is hard to imagine a better and bright future if you don't take time to question the status quo and dare to believe that things can be different in a much better way. Ask questions that open you up to possibilities, and unleash your creativity.

You need to have moments of introspection if you want to get what you want in life.

That is the first bit of asking - asking internally.

Externally, you ask other people. It is an acknowledgement that you need help and that others can provide that help for you.

We all get by in life, like I said, by asking. Asking for favours here and there. There are no self-made people, we need and depend on each other. The President or prime minister to be, for example, will ask the electorate to vote for him/her, the beggar on the streets will ask passers-by for some spare change, and each of us will from time to time ask each other for favours.

By not asking, you short-change your opportunities, you limit yourself, you suffer, and continue to live in mediocrity when things could otherwise be better for you. And to be honest, most of the time, if you don't ask for help, you are the one who will ultimately suffer the most.

Christ said, ask, and it shall be given you..., for everyone who asks receives.

A lot of people, however, find it challenging to ask and would rather suffer in silence than bother with the whole business of asking – that is, asking others for help or support.

Why? Why is that the case?

I think it is because of the following three reasons:

1. Fear
2. Ignorance and
3. Disappointments.

Let's explore those three reasons in a bit more detail, shall we?

No. 1 - FEAR,

We will talk about two types of fear; the fear of secrets being exposed, and the fear of rejection.

Let's look at the fear of secrets being exposed, first.

There is this a notion that we all have 'skeletons in our closets' and some folks are afraid to ask for help even if they are desperate for it for fear that their skeletons will be exposed, and they just cannot stand to bear the shame and humiliation that follows that exposure. For these folks, they would rather suffer in silence than risk humiliation.

Look, here is my advice to you if you fall into this category, fear not. We have all made mistakes in our lives. No one is perfect, and I bet you there is no one who doesn't have the so-called skeletons in his or her closet either.

If you need help, go get it - Ask. Don't let the fear of your past mistakes hold you back from making progress in your life today. There is someone out there who is willing to help you despite the skeletons in your closet. But you have to reach out to them and ask for the help you need.

I hope you got that point. Please reach out and ask for help if you need it and don't be afraid to do so.

Next, is the fear of rejection. This fear has held many, many people back from making progress in their lives! However, the truth of the matter is that nobody will ever be unanimously accepted or liked by everybody in the world, let alone in their own community. And no one has ever been. That would be a real mystery if it happened. So, you see, there is no need to fear rejection.

Come to terms with the fact that some people won't like you for no reason whatsoever! Isn't it strange that something like that happens? Yet it happens all the time in this world we live in.

Should that bother you? Mmm..., no, not really. Some people will reject you no matter what you do, and so there is no point of being bothered by rejections. Just be cool about it, be you, be true to yourself. There are many other people out there who will like you for who you are and who will be willing to lend you a helping hand should you need it.

Your life must go on no matter the rejections which you will inevitably encounter from some people. Do not be put off by them, and neither should the prospect of rejection cause you not to ask for help. Go ahead and ask anyway. If someone rejects your request, move on!

Okay, cool. So, to summarise this section on Fear, here is the deal, do not allow the fear of your past mistakes or the fear of rejection to hold you back from progress. Be bold, be courageous, and ask for help as and when you need it, and keep asking till you get it, someone somewhere, somehow, will help you at some point.

So, if you have been asking for help lately and only to find doors slammed at your face for most of the time, don't lose heart, keep knocking, and keep asking, a door will soon open, and it might be a very big door.

There you have it, Fear is the number one reason why people do not ask for help, and the second reason is ignorance.

No.2- IGNORANCE

Some of us at times have no clue whatsoever that help is available, and because of that ignorance, we ask not and just keep wishing and hoping.

Ignorance is defined as the "lack of knowledge or information".

Ignorance is such a terrible 'disease', and it will keep you in the dark as for long as you accept or embrace it. No wonder in the courts of law they say that "Ignorance is no defence", and I now sort of understand why they say so. The onus is always on you to find out what you don't know.

Think about this for a moment, will you? If you don't know what sort of help is available or where to get it from, how can you ask for it? You are essentially handicapped.

So, how can you ensure that you have access to the key pieces of information you need to make progress and succeed in life?

Here is what you should do, diligently be on the lookout for information and people that can be of help to you.

Get to know who the decision-makers in your neighbourhood are, as well as in your workplace, your social club, your church, etc. Connect with people, network regularly, be outgoing, avoid living in your own little world and embrace the broader community of humanity. It is far easier to get help from people you have a connection with, than from total strangers. I, therefore, urge you to make it your goal in life to be a very well connected person, one that has meaningful and mutually beneficial relationships with other people.

People are your greatest allies in the attainment of your goals. Connect with them, make friends, be genuinely interested in them. It is important that you take this issue of making connections with other people seriously. You see, connections, are like a bridge that facilitates the flow of what you want from the other person to you. It is far easier to get something from somebody you have a connection with, than one you don't. So, don't isolate yourself from society unless you have taken a vow of solitude.

Someone once said that "*Your network is your networth*". And I happen to agree with them. Money travels through relationships. So, make sure that you are well connected, and always be building meaningful and mutually beneficial relationships with others.

Don't be clueless either. Educate yourself, read good books, get to know where to find help should you ever be in need of it. Don't leave things to chance and guesswork. Got it? Wonderful.

Moving on,

No.3 - DISAPPOINTMENTS

The third reason why people do not ask or shall I say don't bother to ask is because of DISAPPOINTMENTS.

Why people do not ask, or shall I say don't bother to ask is that they have asked for far too long and too often without much to show for it, and so they are just tired of asking, and have lost all hope. They are now just getting by in life, wishing and hoping that somehow things will work out for them (fingers crossed).

Oh no, don't do that. That can never be the solution.

By doing so, you surrender a very precious ingredient for successful living - PERSISTENCE

The tragedy of this kind of approach to life is that, by quitting, you relegate yourself to defeatism by an act of your own will. Now, let me ask you this question: Is it worth giving up on your dreams, your aspirations, your hopes, and live a life of mediocrity, pain and misery because you have been disappointed at some point in your life?

Well, if you are truly honest with yourself, your answer will be an emphatic NO! And rightly so. You can't afford to quit because you have had many disappointments in life, no, you mustn't. Hell no!

What you need to do is PERSIST. That's right, hold on, dig in there, persevere right to the end. If what you are after will make a difference in your life and the lives of many other people, hold on to the very end. Do not quit, no matter how many disappointments you meet along the way.

I am reminded at this juncture of one particular story that Jesus Christ told on this very fundamental principle of persistence when he narrated the parable of a widow who presented her case before the unjust Judge. The widow persisted in asking for Justice from the Judge who couldn't care less about her issue or case. But she did not give up, she persisted until the judge finally could not stand her persistence and eventually gave in and helped her. You can find this story in Luke 18:1-6.

The moral here is that; you cannot afford to give up on yourself, however high the stakes are.

Ask in FAITH. Scripture says, "*But when you ask, you must believe and not doubt, because the one who doubts is like a wave of the sea, blown and tossed by the wind. That person should not expect to receive anything from the Lord. Such a person is double-minded and unstable in all they do*" James 1:6-8

Now, asking, is like an art or skill, and like any art or craft, it is 'perfected' through practice. You have to ask with wisdom and prudence and in Faith. You simply can't go about asking carelessly.

You need to ask the right person - one who has the wherewithal to help you. For example, in the story of the widow earlier on, she knew whom to ask help from. She did not go to the doctor, or teacher, she went to the Judge (the person who held the key to the solution she desired – justice). If that person doesn't help as some will probably do, there will be other people you can ask. Just keep asking the right people until you get sorted.

Do not give up.

What you also need to remember is that, in the art of asking, Giving precedes receiving. What does that mean?

Simply this; whenever you ask, be prepared to give before you receive.

Let's face it, until you master the art of giving, the fact is, most of your asking will be in vain. That was true centuries ago, it's still true today and will be true tomorrow.

You have to give. Give what? You may ask. To begin with, give your imagination the chance to work on your desires, don't limit it via doubt.

Secondly, you'll have to give your time, give up your pride, give up your egotism, give up your shame, give up your shyness and yes, sometimes you will even have to spend money to get what you are asking for. And I don't mean bribes here, what I mean, for example is that, you might have to pay some money (give money out) to be trained in a certain skill before you can successfully ask for and get a job. Get what I mean?

There is no question about it, we'll all need assistance from time to time. The question though is this; when you are in that place of need, will you ask for help? Will you let your imagination help you? Will you let others help you?

You decide. The choice is yours.

My closing remarks would be this - **There is no harm in Asking. ASK confidently and ask expectantly and persist till you get what you want.**

Fittingly, I shall defer the last word on this subject to Jesus Christ: He said in Matthew 7:7 *'ASK, and it shall be given you; seek and ye shall find; knock, and it shall be opened unto you: For everyone that asks receives...*"

> *"Be genuinely interested in other people. It is important that you take this issue of making connections with other people seriously. You see, connections, are like a bridge that facilitates the flow of what you want from the other person to you. It is far easier to get something from somebody you have a connection with, than one you don't."*

16

CREATING AWESOME CLARITY IN YOUR LIFE

Be still and know.

The pace at which we are living our lives nowadays is undoubtedly fast compared to that of previous generations, and it is for the greater part characterised by restlessness, anxiety, confusion, and over sensitivity.

Swiftness and urgency seem to be the order of the day, people are constantly rushing here and there, busy with this and that, and given the rate of technological advancement, things across continents are happening at a click of a button. Yeah, that's the world we live in.

It almost seems like if you don't 'keep up with the Joneses', you will wake up one day and find yourself out of touch with civilisation.

Patience, which once used to be a well-cherished virtue seems to have vanished from society, and instead, the instantaneous culture seems to be here to stay.

Someone rightly said one time that; we seem to be living in a ‘microwave' generation, where everything has to be ready in a matter of seconds/minutes.

The wonderful practice of taking time to be quiet, to be still and serene has been so relegated to nothingness in many peoples lives, and no wonder the problems associated with a hectic lifestyle are on the rise the world over, but especially in the advanced economies.

However, to be truly effective in the mid to long term, one must take time to rest, to plan, to strategies, to visualise, and to generally think things through. And you cannot do so, effectively, if you are surrounded with a lot of noise, either externally from your environment or internally from your own state of inward restlessness.

If you carry on subjecting your body and mind to too much strain without adequate periods of rest, for recuperation, it won’t be long before you realise that you can't cope any longer, and if you must cope you will do so at great expense, and your life may well be the ultimate price you’ll pay. That’s quite sombre, isn’t it? You can, however, train yourself to be inwardly quiet, still, and tranquil.

"The more tranquil a man becomes, the greater is his success, his influence, his power for good. Calmness of mind is one of the beautiful jewels of Wisdom" said James Allen.

The practice of stillness or silence as it is sometimes called, will help bring clarity to your life.

So, what exactly is stillness, and how can you benefit from the practicing it?

It's **the art of finding inner peace.** "*Stillness acts as a gateway to the spiritual, a gateway of three successive forms of stillness. The first, stillness of the body-heart-mind, develops in meditation when we sit quietly long enough. The body's fidgeting, itching, and restlessness settle down gradually as it attains rest and stillness. Our heart may recall a situation in life that brings into play one of the many hues of emotion. Or a totally imaginary event in our daydreams calls forth an emotion. But gradually, in quiet meditation, the waves of emotion also settle down to a peaceful state of equanimity. Our brain can be pouring thoughts one over another in a cascading stream. As we watch our thoughts, unmoved, not participating in them, just listening to them pass, they slow down. In some cases, they may cease altogether for periods". Second is Stillness of awareness, stillness of consciousness, and the third one is the stillness of Neither stillness of consciousness, nor stillness of will depend on stillness of the body. Thoughts and emotions can be streaming, the body moving, seeing, hearing, and speaking, and yet, simultaneously, underlying all these more external perceptions, we can stay in touch with the more interior, the stillness of consciousness, open in our will, fully present. Neither stillness of consciousness, nor stillness of will depend on stillness of the body. Thoughts and emotions can be streaming, the body moving, seeing, hearing, and speaking, and yet, simultaneously, underlying all these more external perceptions, we can stay in touch with the more* *interior, the stillness of consciousness, open in our will, fully present.* http://www.innerfrontier.org/Practices/Stillness.htm

Being still or silent is ultimately something that comes from the heart, not from any set of conditions outside us. Living from a place of silence doesn't mean never talking, never engaging or doing things; it simply means that we are not *disturbed* inside; there isn't constant internal chatter. If we're truly silent, then no matter what situation we find ourselves in, we will be at peace.

So, if you desire to have your ways established, and live the kind of life you desire, you will have to make time to practice stillness. If you are to keep sound wisdom and discretion, moments of stillness will be inevitable.

The practice of stillness is the art of Kingship and greatness. Stillness is the element of greatness. It is in Stillness that great things fashion themselves.

Say less, act and listen more. That's the principle here. And the place of effective listening (to yourself and others) is in silence, in stillness. That is where you fine tune your goals and aspirations and create awesome clarity in your life.

It is in these moments of stillness that your desires are fashioned long before they appear in the physical world, it is here that you see the invisible, it is here that you call those things that are not, to being, and it is from this place that you win every battle.

If you become diligent in the practice of stillness, you will grow to love and cherish those quiet moments, and there will be a form of poise, calm and collected disposition about you that will be evident in your character. Furthermore, you will develop your imaginative faculty and sharpen your mental cutting edge.

There is that quiet place where we hear from God, and my submission to you is that, that place is STILLNESS. I recommend that you yearn for it with all your heart and dwell in it when you find it, then return to it as often as you can. "*Be still and know that I am God*", Psalm 46:10.

For some of us, however, moments of stillness are more like a luxury. I don't have the time for that, we say to ourselves. Responsibilities, deadlines, and all sorts of stuff seem to always raise their heads up for attention, and we often give in. We find ourselves dragged here and there, by the so-called - life emergencies.

What a shame that we don't seem to make time for the one thing that could be helpful in averting the occurrence and reoccurrence of the so-called life emergencies, and that thing is – taking time to be still.

Anyway, I have great news for you today my dear friend. You see, all of us have 24 hours in a day, no more, no less. From the richest man to the poorest man alive today, from the strongest to the weakest man, no one gets more than 24 hours daily. Without question, I think that is the one thing you can say is fair and equitable in the whole wide world – The gift of time.

However, how each of us uses this gift, the 24 hours, is where the vast difference in life experiences, and outcomes emanate from. Many people spend their time doing urgent things while altogether neglecting important things, and they seem to have forgotten that urgency does not necessarily mean, or equal importance.

That is why taking time to be quiet and still will help you to remember, and identify what is important visa vee what is urgent. And once you have established that difference, you can then spend a great chunk of your 24 hours doing those important things first. The difference it will make in your life will be stupendous.

Spending time being still can be done in various ways. You could set it up in your daily or weekly routine to have an hour or so to practice stillness.

You could go for a quiet retreat, or journal your thoughts, or do something outside of your normal day to day job, etc. Anything that helps you quiet your mind and relax will do, but the practice of silence is best. And however much time you allocate to being still is up to you, the important thing is that you make time to do so.

Take a moment and listen, take a moment and see, but listen and see from within, in the silence of your heart.

I have personally found that when I spend time being still, my intellect gets sharper and my sense of perception of spiritual realities becomes keener.

Another benefit you will find with being still is that you get to appreciate and be thankful for some of the gifts and good things you've got in your life that you might be taking for granted. And you also tend to look at problems and challenges in a totally new untroubling way. The practice of stillness is really a good thing to do, and a wonderful thing to make a part of your lifestyle.

Now, I am well aware that taking time to be still is easier said than done. I am under no illusion that you can just start this thing today and get on with it and enjoy doing so. No, it is more involved than that – at least in the beginning. You need to work on disciplining your out of control mind, and get yourself together.

If you decide to make stillness and the practice of silence, a part of your lifestyle, then you need to be aware of certain things that will hinder you in making progress, and one of them is the vice of talkativeness - pointless chatter. Yes, that one, we are all prone to it, aren't we?

Expel from yourself the propensity to talk too much, unnecessarily. For in uncontrolled talkativeness lurk the most dreadful passions: lying, loose speech, meaningless chatter, buffoonery, obscenity, and mental fog. To put the matter succinctly; through indiscriminate talkativeness, you rob yourself of the opportunity to be great.

Apostle Paul in his wisdom, knowing the danger that lurks in being indiscriminately talkative, advised his young apprentice and disciple – Timothy, saying: "*...shun profane and vain babblings: for they will increase unto more ungodliness*" 2 Timothy 2:16

And in Proverbs 10:19, the teacher says; *"In the multitude of words, there wanteth not sin: but he who refraineth his lips is wise".* And according to *Matthew 12:36,* Jesus Christ said that *"you will give an account of every idle word that you speak".*

Need I say more? No. It is pretty clear what sort of advice we are being given here, and it is this - *only speak when it is necessary for you to do so, and even then, let your words be few and measured to the occasion and situation.*

Let me close this chapter with the following remark: Today is here, and it's yours to do whatever you want with it, it's a gift, and what you do with it and how you use it, is your business, but there is a price to pay for it's misuse and great rewards await you for its wise use. The ball is in your hands.

I hope you will take some time in your schedule today to be still or start practicing stillness.

17

SELF-MASTERY AND SUCCESS

How to unleash the greatness within you.

If there is one thing that has the most significant impact in scampering your success in life, I would say it is the lack of self-control. That's right, **self-control** is the foundation of self-mastery and is a fundamental part of a healthy, strong, and prosperous life, and the lack of it is sure to be a serious problem if you want to live a life of purpose, impact, and influence, and walk the path of greatness.

The secret to greatness lies in self-mastery and Love. The truth, however, is this: the ability to stay disciplined and hold yourself accountable, is not that easy to consistently uphold in this very fragmented world we live in. A world full of enticing temptations and options that can derail your attempt to be disciplined.

However, the necessity to train yourself to be self-controlled and disciplined must not be neglected if you want to successfully live up to your potential and unleash the greatness within you.

The scriptures do have some very poignant things to say about self-control, and the most telling one for me is in Proverbs 25:28 (ESV), and here is what it says; "*A man without self-control is like a city broken into and left without walls*".

Just pause for a moment and consider that statement again – "*A man without self-control is like a city broken into and left without walls*". Pause and reflect some more.

Here, you have a picture of defeat, destruction, and no protection! Is that how you want your life to look like, or turn out to be? Is it?

Let me leave you to ponder that for a minute or so before we move on. "*A man without self-control is like a city broken into and left without walls*". See the picture, consider the consequences.

Okay, so, you see, self-control is not really an option if you want to be a man or woman of means in this world; if you want to be a great person - one who is strong, confident, courageous, and successful. If you neglect to exercise control over yourself, you can be sure of nothing else, except a very chaotic, messy, and stressful life. That's for sure.

Here then are some areas that I believe you certainly need to gain self-control over in your life.

1. Your Tongue
2. Your Anger
3. Your Thinking
4. Your Desires

Let's begin with;

Your Tongue

By your tongue, I am not referring to that organ in your mouth, no. The tongue is used here as a metaphor for your speech, and as such, taking control of your tongue is about how to control your speech - the way you talk to yourself and other people, the manner and substance of it.

Have you ever heard of this saying: "*Words can build bridges, and they can also build walls*?" O how true.

I know of some people who have not spoken to each other for years because many years ago, some words were said that built invisible walls between them.

I have also read from history archives, the account of wars that were started with words (words of malice, hatred, dissent etc.) and wars that were also won with words, words that inspired courage and confidence in those on the front line.

Your words matter, and it is imperative that you ensure that they are measured and appropriate. Proverbs 18: 21 (ESV) says; "*Death and life are in the power of the tongue, and those who love it will eat its fruits.*"

Control your tongue. Only a fool would consider bubbling whatever is in their mind without due regard to the consequences of their words. The scriptures say in Proverbs 29:11 that "*A fool vents all his feelings, but a wise man holds them back.*" And Proverbs 29:20 echoes it this way; *Do you see someone who speaks in haste? There is more hope for a fool than for them.*"

Look, the Bible has nothing good to say about a fool, yet for it to say that there is more hope for a fool than for somebody who is hasty or too anxious to speak, says volumes about the folly of not having control over your tongue.

For your own sake, keep your tongue under control, will you? There is no need to be hasty with your words. You are bound to make a fool of yourself if you keep on that path. Better to listen more and speak less.

The other aspect of your tongue is the conversations you have within yourself, self-talk as it were. The truth is, we all engage in private conversations with ourselves all the time, and there is nothing you can do about it except to control the direction and nature of that inner conversation. You can no more stop it than you can stop the rising and setting of the sun, it has to happen.

Your challenge then is to make sure that no matter what, you must engage in positive rather than negative self-talk. Train yourself to do so through positive affirmations.

Self-talk affects you in a very deep subconscious level (in your 'creative womb') and as such, what you say to yourself in secret will be reflected in your outer world soon or later.

So be careful about the sort of conversations you indulge in, inwardly. Better still, control those conversations and align them affirmatively to your hopes and dreams in life. The most profound conversations you will have in life are those you will have with yourself.

Do you follow me? I trust you do.

Okay, let's move on and look at the next thing you'll need to exercise self-control over.

Your Anger

How do you control your Anger?

Well, the truth is, many things will happen in your life that will cause you to get angry. First of all, there is nothing wrong with getting angry or upset, we are somewhat built that way. We react and respond to certain things in our lives and in the world around us with anger because we have emotions, and anger is an emotion.

You shouldn't blame yourself or feel bad about getting angry or upset when something causes you to do so. What is not right or okay, however, is the failure to control yourself and thereby let your anger lead you to do some foolish things. That shouldn't be acceptable, and if you let that happen, you are a fool, and you'll have to face the consequences of your actions.

Scripture says in Ephesians 4:26 (KJV) that; "*Be ye angry, and sin not: let not the sun go down upon your wrath.*"

So, be careful, control yourself and do not let your anger drive you to do crazy things you might regret later. Remember, there is nothing wrong with getting angry, just make sure that you control yourself, and maintain your dignity.

And just as a side note; avoid making important decisions or engaging in serious discussions when angry. It is better that you calm yourself down first. Otherwise, I am almost certain that you will come to regret the decision you make under those circumstances.

James, in his epistle, said: "*...let every person be quick to hear, slow to speak, slow to anger; for the anger of man does not produce the righteousness of God.*" James 1:19-20

Don't let yourself down because of your anger, get it under control. Avoid places, people or situations that will exacerbate your anger.

Got it? Okay, let's move on.

Next, let's look at;

Your Thinking.

How do you control your thinking, or make it work for you?

This is another important area of your life that you can't afford to just leave to the whims of your emotions or uncontrolled desires.

Failure to control what you allow yourself to be thinking about will leave you so susceptible to be controlled by external influences, and more to your detriment than benefit.

If you let other people or circumstances control the narrative of what you think, then I can confidently say that you are done. Seriously, what hope is there for you? It is virtually impossible for you to make anything of your life because you are unconsciously letting others inadvertently run your life for you. Your right for self-determination would have been highjacked, and the worst thing would be that you allowed it to happen. Don't go there. Sift through what you hear and see from the news and social media and don't just take in all you hear and see, at face value. Think for your own self, have your own mind.

I always like to refer to the scriptures for guidance, and here is something I would like to offer you from the scriptures about controlling what you think. It is in Philippians 4:8, and it says; "*Finally, brethren, whatsoever things are true, whatsoever things are honest, whatsoever things are just, whatsoever things are pure, whatsoever things are lovely, whatsoever things are of good report; if there be any virtue, and if there be any praise, think on these things.*"

So, whenever you catch yourself starting to drift to the path of distressing and unwholesome thoughts, just remember Philippians 4:8 and quickly change course and focus your mind on to something rather edifying and uplifting. That prerogative is yours, so, use it.

The subject of choosing your thoughts is so important that I have dedicated a whole chapter to it, and I hope you will take some time to study it. The chapter is called; *Here is where people begin to rise and fall.* See the table of contents for the page number.

Okay, so far, we have looked at three vital areas of life that you need to master by exercising self-control; that is, controlling your tongue, your anger, and your thinking. There is one more area we must address, and that is;

Controlling your Desires.

There are three desires I would like to talk about,

The three desires are:

i. The desire for Food

ii. The desire for pleasure and

iii. The desire for Sex

I will focus on two of these desires in this chapter and the third one in the next chapter.

So, let me begin with the desire for food.

This is a biological and very legitimate desire that must be met for the sustenance of life here on earth. However, a lack of self-control in matters related to food can cause all sorts of problems.

You don't have to look very far for evidence of what I am saying here. The health system here in the UK, for example, is so much under strain partly because of food and diet-related illnesses like obesity, diabetes etc.

One of the main reasons why most people have habits that cause or exacerbate diet related illnesses is that most people eat mainly for taste rather than for nourishment. And the commercial sector has wasted no time in capitalising on that. You know how big the fast-food industry is, don't you? Their food certainly tastes great, but I am not that sure of the nutritional value of it compared to other options like for example a home cooked dinner a quality restaurant meal.

Look, I am not saying that you should not eat fast-foods. No, that is not what I am saying. You can eat fast-foods if you want to, but just make sure that you don't make it your main source of food and nourishment.

Another way of making sure that you have discipline over your eating habits is to make sure that you don't always eat to satiety. Resist the temptation to be belly full all the time you eat, instead, just eat what is enough to nourish your body to keep it going till another mealtime.

If you are struggling to understand what the sufficient nourishment would be for yourself, consider using some nutrition apps to help in this area. You can get these apps from the app store for Apple phones, or Google play store for android phones.

Discipline yourself to eat at set times, other than eating as and when you feel like it.

Fasting is also another very good way to learn how to exercise self-control over an excessive desire for food. Fasting not only strengthens your spiritual powers, but it is also very good for your physical health (google the health benefits for fasting and learn more about it). Do, however, consult with your physician or spiritual guide for guidance in this matter.

Don't let your desire and appetite for food go overboard and lead you into all sorts of health problems. You can and should hold yourself accountable for how you nourish your body and how you relate to food. If you don't, well, you will suffer the consequences. Need I say more? No, '*A word is enough for a wise man*', so goes the saying.

Moving on, *we will look at the desire for pleasure next.*

You have probably heard of the 'pleasure-pain' principle, haven't you?

"*The pleasure-pain principle was originated by Sigmund Freud in modern psychoanalysis, although Aristotle noted the significance in his 'Rhetoric', more than 300 years BC. We are born with a pleasure principle, that we will seek immediate gratification of needs, for which our bodies reward us with feelings of pleasure, and the pain principle says that, whilst seeking pleasure people will also seek to avoid pain. The pleasure principle is at the base of hedonism, the idea that life is to be lived to the full and pleasure sought as a primary goal. Hedonists in the extreme will be self-destructive in their use of sex, drugs, rock and roll and other methods of gratification.*" Reference:
http://changingminds.org/disciplines/psychoanalysis/concepts/pleasure_pain.htm

Don't ever underestimate your desire for pleasure. It is such a strong desire and the only thing you can do about it is to control it. You cannot get rid of it. If you choose not to control it and rather go full-on to enjoy yourself without control, you will in no time reduce yourself to poverty and completely sabotage your chances of any success in life.

One effective way I have found of controlling my desire for pleasure is to always heed these words: "*So whether you eat or drink or whatever you do, do it all for the glory of God.*" 1 Corinthians 10:31 (NIV). (And God is within you).

To be honest, I don't always succeed in living up to the words of that scripture all the time, and wherever that happens, and I get convicted in my heart, I repent and change course in a positive direction. But also, whenever I have put those words into practice, it sure did prove to be the right thing to do. I commend *1 Corinthians 10:31* to you too, and here it is: – "*So whether you eat or drink or whatever you do, do it all for the glory of God."* And remember that the Kingdom of God is within you.

Just before we move on and consider the desire for Sex, let us wrap up what we have so far considered in this chapter on Self-Control, and talk about Greatness, from James Allen: "*The great man has become such by the scrupulous and unselfish attention to small duties. He has become wise and powerful by sacrificing ambition and pride in the doing of those necessary things which evoke no applause and promise no reward. He never sought greatness; he sought faithfulness, unselfishness, integrity, truth; and in finding these in the common round of small tasks and duties, he unconsciously ascended to the level of greatness.*

The great man knows the vast value that inheres in moments, words, greetings, meals, apparel, correspondence, rest, work, detached efforts, fleeting obligations, in the thousand-and-one little things which press upon him for attention-briefly, in the common details of life. He sees everything as divinely apportioned, needing only the application of dispassionate thought and action on his part to render life blessed and perfect. He neglects nothing, does not hurry; seeks to escape nothing but error and folly; attends to every duty as it is presented to him, and does not postpone and regret. By giving himself unreservedly to his nearest duty, forgetting alike pleasure and pain, he attains to that combined childlike simplicity and unconscious power which is ***greatness****.*

Self-control is the pathway to Greatness.

Let's move on and look at the desire for sex next, and I have dedicated the whole of the next chapter to talk about this desire.

> *The ability to discipline and hold yourself accountable is not that easy to consistently uphold. However, the necessity to train yourself to be self-controlled and disciplined must not be neglected if you want to successfully live up to your potential.*

18

THE DESIRE FOR SEX AND HOW TO USE IT POSITIVELY

"So strong and impelling is the desire for sexual contact that people freely run the risk of life and reputation to indulge in it".
Napoleon Hill.

The sex drive is one of the most powerful stimuli of the human mind, very close to the survival instinct – the desire to live.

There is obviously nothing wrong with either of these desires, after all, the creator himself programmed them into humans and the animals alike. He obviously put them there for a reason.

The desire for sex expression is the most powerful of all human desires and a very strong stimulant of the mind. And because of the limited knowledge most people have about the sexual desire, the state of mind created by this powerful emotion is generally associated with the physical act.

"*So strong and impelling is the desire for sexual contact that people freely run the risk of life and reputation to indulge in it,*" said Napoleon Hill.

And because of the improper influences to which people have been subjected to in acquiring knowledge of sex, things essentially physical have biased the mind.

You've probably heard of well-documented accounts of prominent people, especially men, who have let this powerful e

motion lead them to do things that brought their offices, positions, and reputations to disrepute.

History is littered with the accounts of politicians, clergymen, celebrities, and ordinary people alike who completely lost control of this emotion and desire and in doing so have wrecked their lives so to say.

Sex has very constructive potentialities; humankind, for example, would not be perpetuated without it. Extensive research by leading institutions and professors have led us to believe that sex is very good for the maintenance of health (as a therapeutic agency, it has no equal).

The sexual emotion is also a great stimulant, and when driven by it, one gets very charged up for action and feels powerful.

And "*Because the sex drive is so powerful and basic to human existence, information about sex is ever popular. The media has homed in on this, and the sex industry - arguably one of the biggest - is a great money-spinner. Countless books, magazines, newspapers, radio broadcasts, TV shows, films, videos, tapes, compact disks, and dedicated sex shops are linked to the sex industry: endlessly feeding the public with sex-oriented material. I do not need to elaborate on this fact; because everyone knows that sex is big business - all over the world!"* https://www.joybysurprise.com/sex-and-the-bible.html

And here is the sad part, this divinely programmed urge has been corrupted and abused by mankind down through the ages. All sorts of sexual perversions are on display all around us. You don't really have to dig deep or do extensive research to notice it.

However - and you had better sit down for this - it turns out that, this mighty emotion and stimulant can be redirected by switching the mind from thoughts of physical expression to thoughts of some other nature.

The thing is, the emotion of sex contains the secret to creative ability.

Destroy the sex glands, whether in man, or any other animal and you would have removed a major cause of action, and you can prove this by observing what happens to any animal after it has been castrated, a bull for example, becomes as docile as a cow after it's been castrated. Whether in beast or human, destroying the sex glands alters their hormonal balance in such a way that the fight that was in them is all taken.

The sex drive is there for a reason, and when harnessed and redirected along other lines, the positive attributes of this powerful desire has the potential of being used as a power for creativity in a profession or calling.

You can channel your sexual energy to works of literature, and art. You can also channel it in physical workouts in a gym to develop a strong body and muscles.

Redirecting your sexual energy in these ways is a process that Napoleon Hill called Sex Transmutation, in his book – Think and Grow Rich.

Napoleon Hill went further to say that: "*The transmutation of sex energy calls for the exercise of will power, to be sure, but the reward is worth the effort.*

The desire for sexual expression is inborn and natural. The desire cannot and should not be submerged or eliminated. But it should be given an outlet through forms of expression that enrich the body, mind, and spirit. If not given this form of outlet, through transmutation, it will seek outlets through purely physical channels.

A river may be dammed, and its water controlled for a time, but eventually, it will force an outlet. The same is true of the emotion of sex. It may be submerged and controlled for a time, but its very nature causes it to be ever seeking means of expression. If not transmuted into some creative effort, it will find a less worthy outlet.

Fortunate indeed, are those who have discovered how to give sex emotion an outlet through some form of creative effort, for they have, by discovery, lifted themselves to the status of the genius."

People are influenced in their actions not by cold reason so much as by 'feelings'. The creative faculty of the mind is set into action entirely by emotions, not by cold reason, and the most powerful of all human emotions is that of sex. There are other mind stimulants, but none of them, nor all of them combined, can equal the driving power of SEX."

I remember when I was in my twenties and highly sex driven, my safety zone was the gym. I used to take my sexual energy and use it to sculpt my body in the gym. And it worked, I didn't find myself messing about with ladies, though the temptation was ever present. And most people also used to remark on how amazing my body looked.

It was also at the same time that I started writing blog posts of which big chunks are now part of this very book you hold in your hands. I learnt the art of sex transmutation, and it kept me out of trouble, I channelled that energy into other worthy causes. And even now that I am married, I don't overindulge in it, because I have trained myself well, and so can you.

Like I said before, the subject of Sex is one which most people have limited their knowledge and interest just to its physical expression. The urge for sex has been so misunderstood, exaggerated by the ignorant and ill-informed for far too long so much so that the very mention of the word sex triggers all sorts of suspicions and raised eyebrows (it's almost like a taboo that you don't talk about such things) and yet secretly, they love to indulge in it.

The sex drive should be used intelligently and with discrimination. It should not be used to such an extent that it debases rather than enrich both body and mind, and the key to ensuring that, that doesn't happen is to avoid intemperance and practice the art of sex transmutation.

Intemperance in sexual habits is just as detrimental as intemperance in habits of eating or drinking.

Overindulgence in sexual activity may lead to a very destructive habit and may well be as detrimental as narcotics in hampering your creative efforts, because you will be misusing your creative energy by overindulging it in sex.

Uncontrolled sexual desires expressed indiscriminately have the potential to wreck your life and sabotage your dreams and success in life. If you are one of those people who happen to have been endowed with a high sex drive, I would like to talk to you for a minute. Listen, there are so many other ways you can use your sexual drive than just in the way people are accustomed to. You can channel it creatively to enrich yourself and the world around you, through art, literature, sport, music etc.

Don't be one of those people who will be numbered in the history archives - private or public, for failing to control their sexual appetite, and subsequently go down in history with shame on your back, not for being highly sex driven, but for misusing your sexual drive. I am sure you can do better. I have faith in you because you are reading this book.

Look, the sex drive is there for a reason beyond its use for physical sexual activity, and you will do well to learn the art of sex transmutation to redirect that sex energy to more edifying ends that will enrich and not debase yourself. You will be glad you did it. Avoid situations and circumstances that have the potential to exacerbate your sexual appetite and cause you to put it in unprofitable use; things like pornography and flirting around. Don't go there.

19

HERE IS WHERE PEOPLE BEGIN TO RISE AND FALL

"Whether you think you can, or you think you can't—you're right."
Henry Ford

It is just as essential to know how to think correctly as it is to know how to speak or act correctly.

Regardless of whether or not you translate your thoughts into actual performance, the thoughts themselves would have already produced some kind of effect in your life.

Your thoughts are so powerful so much so that your character and outlook in life today are a result of your thinking over the years.

Make no mistake; your thinking is always shaping you. Thinking is a creative force that is constantly at work in humanity. Thinking is one of those things that we have no option as humans but to do. Everybody thinks. The only difference in people's thinking is what they think about. And the good news is that you have the power to choose your thoughts!

The big question then is this; what will you be thinking about or rather, what will you choose to think about?

In the final analysis, your success or failure is ultimately of your own making. And the person at the centre of everything that happens to, and for you, is YOU! God provides guidance, and you make the decisions. You should, therefore, be deliberate about what you think, and you should do so on purpose. This is because you will eventually reflect or manifest your thoughts. It is that simple.

And the thing about thoughts is that they compel us to act in accordance with their nature. Whether those be fearful and death inducing thoughts, or courageous and life affirming thoughts.

In the scripture below, we are all encouraged to think aright. Here is what it says: "*Finally, brethren, whatsoever things are true, whatsoever things are honest, whatsoever things are just, whatsoever things are pure, whatsoever things are lovely, whatsoever things are of good report; if there be any virtue, and if there be any praise,* ***think on these things.*** Philippians 4:8

Wow! This is beautiful! These are very wonderful things to think about!

Imagine your life turning out like everything apostle Paul mentions in the scripture above, that would be really great! Wouldn't it? Think about it; an honest life, a just life, having a pure conscience, being surrounded by loveliness 365 days of the year, having good things without end, living a virtuous life, and being celebrated. Wow! Wouldn't you love that kind of life? I would.

But then much of our life experience tells us otherwise, right? Of course, it does.

Why is that so?

I believe one of the reasons why we find ourselves not living the way apostle Paul admonishes us to do in the scripture above is because we take ourselves too seriously, so much so that when things don't add up in our lives, (which is quite common) we start thinking and imagining the worst, and that eventually leads to the worst happening! For whatsoever you think about and vividly imagine to be true, will manifest in your life, it will find ways and means you know not of, to do so. Thinking so much about what you don't want to happen in your life, for example, will most likely lead to that very thing happening.

Therefore, be thinking and vividly imagining the things you want to see happen in your life instead. That way, you channel your latent power of thought and potential to great means and ends. Think BIG, renew your mind, and be transformed, that's what the scriptures tell us to do in Romans 12:2 - '*Do not conform any longer to the pattern of this world, but be transformed by the renewing of your mind*'.

So, imagine great things for yourself and then believe

you can have them, then go ahead and prepare to receive them. Think BIG.

Stand guard at the door of your mind, for **it is in your thinking that you will begin to rise or fall.** What you permit to enter your mind and dwell there, will determine what, and how your life turns out to be.

And remember you can change anything at the point of thought. Let me say that again; *You can change anything at the point of thought.* You might be miles away on a wrong path in your life, but a moment of reflective thinking might halt your progress in that path and change the whole trajectory of your journey and destiny in life for the better. The story of the prodigal son as told by Jesus Christ is a perfect example of what I have just said, see *Luke 15:11-32.*

If you want to learn more, think better thoughts, and be wise in life, be willing to suspend your personal beliefs about things, set aside any prejudices and think with an open mind. Anything is possible. You are created in the image and likeness of God, and the essence of God in you is not limited, but you can limit it in your life through your thinking without actually knowing that you are doing so. So, watch your thoughts, and most importantly, choose to think as apostle Paul says in Philippians 4:8.

James Allen in his book – AS A MAN THINKETH (1903) articulated some very profound remarks about thoughts, and I would like to share some of those remarks with you here.

He said, "*The aphorism 'As a man thinketh in his heart so is he' not only embraces the whole of man's being but is so comprehensive as to reach out to every condition and circumstance of his life. A man is literally what he thinks, his character being the complete sum of all his thoughts.*

A noble Godlike character is not a thing of favour or chance but is the natural result of continued effort in right thinking, the effect of long-cherished association with Godlike thoughts.

Man is made or unmade by himself; in the armoury of thought, he forges the weapons by which he destroys himself, he also fashions the tools with which he builds for himself heavenly mansions of joy and strength and peace.

A man's mind may be likened to a garden, which may be intelligently cultivated or allowed to run wild; but whether cultivated or neglected, it must, and will bring forth. If no useful seeds are put into it, then an abundance of useless weed seeds will fall therein and will continue to produce their kind. Let a man radically alter his thoughts, and he will be astonished at the rapid transformation it will effect in the material conditions of his life. Men imagine that thought can be kept secret, but it cannot; it rapidly crystallises into habit, and habit solidifies into circumstance.

Bestial thoughts crystallise into habits of drunkenness and sensuality, which solidify into circumstances of destitution and disease.

Impure thoughts of every kind crystallise into enervating and confusing habits, which solidify into distracting and adverse circumstances.

Thoughts of fear, doubt, and indecision crystallise into weak, unmanly, and irresolute habits, which solidify into circumstance of failure, indigence, and slavish dependence.

Lazy thoughts crystallise into habits of uncleanliness and dishonesty, which solidify into circumstances of foulness and beggary.

Hateful and condemnatory thoughts crystallise into habits of accusation and violence, which solidify into circumstances of injury and persecution.

Selfish thoughts of all kinds crystallise into habits of self-seeking, which solidify into circumstances more or less distressing. On the other hand, beautiful thoughts of all kinds crystallise into habits of grace and kindliness, which solidify into genial and sunny circumstances.

Pure thoughts crystallise into habits of intemperance and self -control, which solidify into circumstances of repose and peace.

Thoughts of courage, self-reliance, and decision crystallise into manly habits, which solidify into circumstances of success, plenty, and freedom.

Energetic thoughts crystallise into habits of cleanliness and industry, which solidify into circumstances of pleasantness.

Gentle and forgiving thoughts crystallise into habits of gentleness, which solidify into protective and preservative circumstances.

Loving and unselfish thoughts crystallise into habits of self-

forgetfulness for others, which solidify into circumstances of sure and abiding prosperity and true riches.
A particular train of thought persisted in, be it good or bad, cannot fail to produce its results on the character and circumstances. A man cannot directly choose his circumstances, but he can choose his thoughts, and so indirectly, yet surely, shape his circumstances.

Nature helps every man to the gratification of the thoughts which he most encourages, and opportunities are presented which will most speedily bring to the surface both the good and evil thoughts.

Let man cease from his sinful thoughts, and all the world will soften toward him, and be ready to help him. Let him put away his weakly and sickly thoughts and lo! Opportunities will spring on every hand to aid his strong resolves. Let him encourage good thoughts, and no hard fate shall bind him down to wretchedness and shame. The world is your kaleidoscope, and the varying combinations of colours which at every succeeding moment it presents to you are exquisitely adjusted pictures of your ever-moving thoughts.

There is no physician like cheerful thought for dissipating the ills of the body; there is no comforter to compare with good will for dispersing the shadows of grief and sorrow. To live continually in thoughts of ill will, cynicism, suspicion, and envy is to be confined in a self-made prison hole. But to think well of all, to be cheerful with all, to patiently learn to find the good in all – such unselfish thoughts are the very portals of heaven; and to dwell day by day in thoughts of peace toward every creature will bring abounding peace to their possessor.

Thought and Purpose.

Until thought is linked to purpose there is no intelligent accomplishment. With the majority the bark of thought is allowed to 'drift' upon the ocean of life. Aimlessness is a vice, and such drifting must not continue for him who would steer clear of catastrophe and destruction.

They who have no central purpose in their life fall easy prey to petty worries, fears, troubles, and self-pitying's, all which are indications of weakness which lead to failure, unhappiness, and loss, for weakness cannot persist in a power-evolving universe.

A man can conceive of a legitimate purpose in his heart and set out to accomplish it. He should make this purpose the centralising point of his thoughts. It may take the form of a spiritual ideal, or it may be a worldly object, according to his nature at the time being. But whichever it is, he should steadily focus his thought forces upon the object which he has set before him. He should make this purpose his supreme duty, and should devote himself to its attainment, not allowing his thoughts to wander away into ephemeral fancies, longings, and imaginings. Even if he fails again and again to accomplish his purpose (as he necessarily must until weakness is overcome), the strength of character gained will be the measure of his true success, and this will form a new starting point for future power and triumph.

Those who are not prepared for apprehension of great purpose should fix their thoughts upon faultless performance of their duty, no matter how insignificant their task may appear. Only in this way can the thoughts be gathered and focused, and resolution and energy be developed which being done, there is nothing which may not be accomplished.

To put away aimlessness and weakness, and to begin to think with purpose, is to enter the ranks of those strong ones who only recognise failure as one of the pathways to attainment, who make all conditions serve them, and who think strongly, attempt fearlessly, and accomplish masterfully.

Having conceived of his purpose, a man should mentally mark out a straight pathway to its achievement, looking neither to the right nor left. Doubts and fears should be rigorously excluded; they are disintegrating elements which break up the straight line of effort, rendering it crooked, ineffectual, useless. Thoughts of doubt and fear never accomplish anything, and never can. They always lead to failure. Purpose, energy, power to do, and all strong thoughts cease when doubt and fear creep in.

He who has conquered doubt and fear has conquered failure. His every thought is allied with power, and all difficulties are bravely met and wisely overcome. His purposes are seasonably planted, and they bloom and bring forth fruit which does not fall prematurely to the ground.

Thought allied fearlessly to purpose becomes creative force."

Peace and Love to you. Dare to think big and rule your world.

> *If you want to learn more and be wise in life, be willing to suspend your personal beliefs about things, set aside any prejudices and think with an open mind. Anything is possible.*

20

THE ONE ESSENTIAL

What one thing would you do if you knew that doing it would make all other things a lot easier, faster, or unnecessary to do?

Have you ever heard of the 80/20 rule? The pareto principle, which states that for many phenomena, 80% of the result comes from 20% of the effort. Ever heard of it?

Well, I want you for now to forget about that because if the 1/0 rule is not complied with, the pareto principle will be meaningless.

What is the 1/0 rule? Well, that is the one or nothing rule, it is the one thing or nothing else matters rule, and I call it the - **The One Essential.** Ever heard of it?

Here is the thing, if haven't yet, soon or later, you will come to the realisation that not all things are equal, and as such, not all things demand the same level of attention and resources.

In virtually all aspects of life, there is always one thing, or one rule or principle that stands out above all others and almost demands that you pay attention to it or else, it won't really matter that much what else you do, because it will be a waste of time.

Consider for example your **business, your work, or career,** what do you think the one essential here is?

Well, the one essential thing here is – **Profit** (added value).

Look, if you are not profitable in your business, you'll be out of business pretty soon. And if you don't find your work profitable, soon or later it will be meaningless to you. And if it is in your job, lack of added value here (profits) will eventually lead you to be given matching orders, that is, fired from your job in no time.

A business that is not profitable soon loses the ability to fund innovation, growth, skills development and quality service or product delivery, because there is no surplus cash. And even lenders will back off if your business is not profitable.

So, ensure that you are profitable in your business, in your work, or in your career. Add value as much as you can.

Next, what do you think is the one essential in **building Wealth(financial)**? Well, that would be to **earn/make money and then spend less than you earn, and wisely invest what you keep.** And what will help you spend less than you earn is the self discipline of **budgeting** your expenses so as to spend less than you earn. Don't spend what you don't have via punitive lines of credit if you can help it. You will never build wealth if you spend all you earn and even more via credit cards.

Money troubles and all sorts of other troubles in the world today, are somewhat linked to the violation of this one essential principle about money. People spend what they don't have. Imagine that! Terrible. You know, I did it too, many years ago, and lived to regret what I had done to myself, big time. I was like a slave, earning, mostly to pay what I owed. That was bad. Gosh, thank God I am no longer in that position and I would urge you not to spend more than you earn through credit if you can help it. Don't do it.

Budgeting should become your friend. You see, when you neglect to account for your expenses and to know where your money goes, you are basically operating on the blind and groping about in the dark, and big ugly surprises await you around the corner, and you will meet them soon or later. However, budgeting helps you operate in the light and helps you decide in advance how your money is put to work productively, and ensuring that you stay in positive cash flow territory as opposed to negative cash flow.

Moving on, what about **learning**? Whether it is learning a skill or anything else, what's the one essential thing you should embrace in learning? Well, that would be – **Consistency**. Nothing beats consistency in learning anything you want to master, You must be consistent in learning it. Keep at it.

What about **friendship**, what do you think is the one essential thing about friendship?

That would be **loyalty**. Nothing else will matter in your friendships if you are so disingenuous and chuck your friends at any moment of trouble. If you want friends, be a friend, be loyal to your friend(s), otherwise you will live a lonely life though surrounded by people.

And **marriage**? What is the one essential thing about it? Wow! This is a big one. I am married, and I can tell you that the one essential thing in marriage is **harmony**. Yes, that's right, harmony is the one essential thing in marriage. You have to do all you can to maintain the spirit of harmony in your marital relationship, no matter the arguments and disagreements that may crop up from time to time. Do all you can to return to a state of harmony. Ignore to do so and pretty soon, you will have no marriage even if you continue living together. What about **life** itself? What is the one essential thing about life?

Well, don't look far, it is in the scriptures, and it is **LOVE**. Love is the one indisputable essential thing about life. Love for yourself, love for your fellow human beings, Love for nature, love for your work, etc. Try life without love, and you may as well vacate the earth. The greatest power in life is Love.

What about **leadership**? How on earth would we be able to operate as communities and nations without leaders? Leadership is sacrosanct for orderly living, but any sensible leader will concur that to lead well, you must be a servant. So, there you have it, the one essential thing about **leadership** is **servanthood**. Want to be a great leader? Have a servants heart.

Moving on, what about **taking action** to achieve something, what is the one essential thing there?

Well, if you seriously think about it, you'll concur with me that it is, **Planning**.

You see, as important as taking action to realise your dreams is, acting on something important in your life without a plan is really nuts. Don't do it. It is a waste of time. You are better off having **a well-prepared plan** of action, as an essential part of **doing anything** to achieve your goals, than just doing stuff without a plan.
What about if you **want to change and transform the way you live your life**, what is the one essential thing you need to do?

Well, that would be **the renewing of your mind**. The scripture puts it this way in Romans 12:2; "*Do not conform to the pattern of this world but be transformed by the renewing of your mind*". In other words, if there is no renewal of your mind, then no transformation takes place either. And your thinking plays a huge role in the renewing of your mind. And it is also true, that you can't generally rise in life above the level of your thinking. So, if you want to rise higher in life, first rise higher in your thinking. Need I say more? No. **Renewing your mind** is the one essential thing about **life transformation**. "*Your mind is your biggest gold mine*" So said Louis King – Managing Director for First Boston Capital Markets, so, renew it often.

Next, let's move on to **conversations**. What do you think is the one essential thing about conversations?

Well, think about this for a moment; have you ever been rudely interrupted by somebody in a conversation because they did not have the intelligence or the courtesy to let you have your say? And if so, how did you feel about that interruption? I am sure you felt perhaps like getting a padlock and locking their mouth. Well, alright, that's a bit dramatic, but I guess you get my point, right?

Now, flip that around and ask yourself whether you have ever rudely interrupted somebody in a conversation, and chances are, you have!
Anyway, if you want to have great conversations, **listen**. Listen to the other party, understand them, then speak. And there you have it – **Patient listening.** Yes, that is the one essential thing about **conversations.** If the other party in the conversation is an impatient bubbler, politely request that they refrain from doing so (bubbling), and if your request is not heeded, excuse yourself from the conversation.

How about **negotiations**? Have you ever been in a situation during a negotiation where you felt like your hands were tied and the only option available to you was to give in?

Well, when this kind of thing happens in negotiations, the real issue is that you have no credible options including the option of walking away should the terms of the offer in the negotiation not be favourable to you.

You need to **have real credible options** at hand to fall back to when going to a negotiation – and that's the one essential thing about negotiations – Having credible options to fall back on. Failure to have options will see you squeezed from every side. Don't put yourself in that position.

And how can you create options? Well, get as much information as you can about what you want to do, therein will lie the options for you.

Okay. Moving on, let's now consider **weight management,** and what its one essential thing is.

The truth is, many people are struggling with their body weight and have done so for many, many years. Talking about weight issues is tricky business because it evokes all sorts of emotions in the people concerned.

If you have weight issues, it is almost certainly true that what goes through your mouth to your stomach (the food you eat – the quality and quantity of it) is very much responsible for your weight problems. But yet again, you see, you are the one responsible for nourishing yourself, and, therefore, the responsibility for your weight issues, squarely lie with you! It is a bit of tough love here, but this has to be said, and I hope you will take what I say here in good faith if you are struggling with your weight at present. I mean well.

Now, here is what I suggest you do to help yourself with weight management, and I believe it to be the one essential thing about weight management, it is this; **eat the right food, at the right time, in the right quantities,**

and exercise your body regularly, and avoid comfort eating. This is only my opinion, but if you need professional advice, and guidance, please seek the help of a competent professional on weight management issues.

There are of course other things you can do to manage your weight, but your eating habits are the place to start from. Eat to nourish your body and not just because the food tastes good. And deal with the emotional scars that may perhaps be causing you to find comfort in food.

And last, and by no means the least is **You.** Yes, you, the person reading these lines right now. What do you think is the one essential thing about You?

Well, it is this: to **understand that you matter, that you have a purpose, being authentically true to yourself and living your life the best way you can without pretending to be somebody else or trying to please everybody in order to fit in or be accepted by others.**

Now, many things might happen to you during the course of your life that may sometimes cause you to wonder whether you really matter. People may say all sorts of things to discredit you, or you might even have abuse hurled at you, perhaps you are currently being treated or have been treated like you are a nobody, and so on, and so forth. Many other things may be going on that might cause you to question and say, what is the point? What am I doing here?

You know what, I totally get it. But here is the thing; do you think you are here by accident? Heck no! I don't think so. You are here for a purpose, and I know you matter. You are a somebody and not a nobody, and unless you understand that, some people will take you for a ride, especially the bullies, and you will just cower in, believing that you are a nobody. Understanding that you matter, that you are somebody, will help you discover your purpose(s) in life and help you find fulfilment, otherwise, nothing else will truly matter.

Finally, the one essential about everyday living is:.... drum roll pleeeaase....., it is **Wisdom**. Wisdom is the principle thing, **get it**. Everyday will require you to make decisions, do things, say things, see things, and without wisdom, your life is bound to be really tough, for sure. And what is wisdom? Wisdom is the right practical application of knowledge. And where do you get wisdom from? You get it from life, by living, by taking action, and by being present – being in the now.

> *In virtually all aspects of life, there is always one thing, or one rule or principle that stands out above all others and almost demands that you pay attention to it or else, it won't really matter that much what else you do, because it will be a waste of time.*

21

HOW TO AVOID REGRETS IN YOUR LIFE

Why you shouldn't take anything or anyone for granted in your life.

You have probably read and received lots of advice about things you should do to be successful, and I have given some of it myself in this book.

But what I want to do in this chapter is to talk to you about taking things for granted and why you shouldn't do it if you want to be successful or continue to be successful in your life. Essentially, I will be talking to you about how to avoid regrets in your life by not taking things for granted.

I will be giving you some principles that can help you maintain a sense of awe and appreciation for the things you already have while at the same time satisfy your curiosity for what is out there. I will also give you information that will help you find ways to fulfil the desire for those things you crave, without taking for granted what you already have.

Let me begin by asking you a question. Have you ever heard of the phrase – *Over familiarity breeds contempt*?

The term "*familiarity*" here, means "overexposure", and "*contempt*" is used in the sense of lack of appreciation or respect, or having disdain.

Generally, it is hard(er) to go on with high degrees of awe and respect for people or things that you encounter *frequently* and have gotten so used to. That encapsulates what the phrase over familiarity is all about, in that, over time, the known and increasingly familiar may desensitise an individual to the initial wonder, respect and awe of the new event, person, or objects that initially increased their attention level and appreciation.

As familiarity grows, and the awe, wonder and appreciation fade, one is almost likely to start devaluing the event, person, or object they once held in awe. In some cases, this devaluation process can open the door to denigration, which may then feed a growing feeling of contempt.

Haven't you noticed, for example, that, the more familiar you get with somebody, the more likely you are to start dwelling on their faults and criticize them?
This is a classic pattern of denigration that may lead to contempt.

I have experienced the dangers of over familiarity play out in my life, and it is certainly the case in many people's lives too, all over the world.

It's all too easy to become laid back once the novelty of what was once captivating, exciting, and awe-inspiring wears off. Over familiarity, leading to increasingly casual or sloppy usage and care is all too common and is the precursor for the deadly habit of **taking things for granted.**

The main problem with us seems to be that we are constantly craving things that we do not have, and for some reason, pay little or no attention to the things we already have. And once we get what we are craving for, another thing takes its place, and the thing we wanted in the first place quickly loses its value – we become so familiar with it, so to say.

We tend to take for granted many things in our lives. For example, we take for granted the food we eat, the water we drink, our health, the people we love, our natural world (nature), our success, and our time on this earth.

Here is the thing though, when you take anything for granted, you are more than likely to lose it, and unless that is your plan, I suggest you think twice before starting to take anything for granted, especially those things in your life.

You see, the human tendency of taking things for granted is common, and the temptation is ever-present. It is so easy to take things for granted.

And again, it goes without saying that you risk losing anything you take for granted, be it your job, your relationships, your business, etc. You don't want that happening to you, do you? I hope not. So, don't take your wife, husband, or partner for granted, don't take your friendships for granted, don't take your job or business for granted. As a matter of fact, take nothing for granted.

Why?

Because it will cost you, and cost you big, really BIG! And **you will regret it**.

Now, I want to assume that you have a solution-oriented approach to life, and with that in mind, I would like to give you four principles that can help you stay grounded, and appreciative of what you have and avoid taking things for granted and thereby avoid regrets in your life.

Here they are:

1. Principle number one is - **Giving thanks.**

Be grateful and give thanks for big and small things in your life. Count your blessings and name them one by one.

Giving thanks releases you from guilt, jealousy, envy and shuts the doors to the complaining, criticising, and condemnatory attitude, which would otherwise cause your life to be a 'living hell', so to say.

Giving thanks should not only be your lifestyle but your nature. This Bible scripture puts it beautifully and remarks it as God's will for your life. It says, "*Rejoice evermore, pray without ceasing, in everything give thanks, for this is the will of God in Christ Jesus Concerning you.* 2 Thessalonians 5:16–18

Giving thanks is characteristic of an attitude of humility, and with such an attitude, it is difficult to take anything for granted.

2. The second principle is – **Growing in Knowledge and Understanding.**

Strive to increase your knowledge and understanding of the people, and things around you. Understand for example, your spouse, your job, your friends or associates, your business, your religion, etc.

And remember that it takes almost a lifetime to sort of fully understand all that there is about a person and some things in life. This is because revelation is progressive with no seeming end in sight. The full spectrum of the absolute truth of most things is not likely to be humanly possible to know, and that is why I caution you against being complacent about learning.

You should always strive to know more of the people and the things around you and your work. *Be committed to growth.* Inquire earnestly, ask questions and search for answers, live a life of adventure! That way, you will never lose PASSION and interest in life, or start taking things for granted.

Growing in knowledge and understanding will help you know the value of something while it is still in your hands, it also does draw you closer to that thing. Some people have gotten to know the value of something when it is too late, i.e., when they have lost it.

When you grow in knowledge and understanding about something you have, it helps avert your 'short-sightedness which would otherwise obscure you from seeing the big picture. It is also worth noting that the more you grow in the knowledge about that thing you have, the more interesting and fascinating that thing becomes to you, and you are then able to look at it at different angles and appreciate it more deeply. Now tell me, why would you take anything like that for granted? Something that is revealing more and more of its wonders to you, why would you like to take it for granted? I suppose you wouldn't.

3. The third principle is about having – **Having Quiet times,** moments of stillness.

What this calls for is taking 'time out' to 'be alone'. This is where you recharge your 'batteries' so to say and get a good perspective about life. You also get to evaluate and analyse issues that concern you, and also attempt to give your dreams a head start. This is what I call

time.

During this time, you get to have a deep appreciation for your life, you look at where you have come from, the people you have met along the way, the challenges and triumphs you have encountered, and you count your blessings and be thankful for all that is, and is to come.

The practice of having Quiet times has the effect of clarifying your vision in life, it also has the effect of opening the 'eyes' of your understanding and of positively influencing and lifting your mood.

Make no mistake, it is in your moments of silence where great things fashion themselves!

4. **Don't judge by Appearances**, is the fourth principle.

Appearances can be very deceptive, and you risk losing out big time if you are more apt to judge things by what you see rather than by facts, and your intuition or gut instinct as it is popularly called.

I think this phrase sums it up perfectly; "*Don't judge a book by its cover.*" And I also like this Bible verse in John 7:24 from the New Living Translation, it says; "*Look beneath the surface so you can judge correctly.*"

You see, the likelihood of you taking something for granted and having regrets later on is increased many times over if you often judge things by appearances. Many people, for example, have entered into terrible relationships because their judgement was based on appearances, and others have missed out on really great relationships, for the same reason – judging by appearances. Great business deals and careers have been missed because of poor judgement based solely on appearances. The list goes on, and on, of opportunities missed because of poor judgements (decisions) that were made based on appearances.

So, resist the urge or temptation to judge things or people by appearances but instead get the facts and base your judgement on those facts or better still, on your intuition. And the well-developed your intuition is, the better and reliable judge it will be.

Moments of stillness and communion with God will help you develop your intuitive prowess.

Those are the four principles to live by, to help you not to take things for granted and avoid regrets in your life. Let me recapitulate.

1. *Giving thanks,*
2. *Growing in Knowledge and understanding*
3. *Having Quiet times*
4. *Not judging by appearances but rather by facts and intuition*

I recommend that you adapt and use the above four principles in your life daily to help you live a rich, successful, fulfilling, and enjoyable life, and not take anything for granted.

Fittingly, the last chapter in this book is about things I wish I learnt earlier in my life, and they are encapsulated in what I call – Thought Provoking Anthology. Let's check them out.

22

THOUGHT PROVOKING ANTHOLOGY

It is important in life that you learn from the past, make the most of today, and optimistically look forward to tomorrow.

I want to wrap up this book with an anthology which I hope you will find both thought-provoking and inspiring.

Here I am, in a Starbucks coffee shop. I have just been in church this morning and felt like having a latte after that roaring sermon in church. The atmosphere in here is chilled out and relaxed, lively music is playing in the background, and it is quite busy with people walking in and out. Those who are seated seemed to be having a good time and chatting to one another. I can see some people reading, others are on their phones and laptops, the smell of the various aromas of coffee is permeating the air in a very refreshing way and it is sunny outside. I have just taken a sip of my latte, and Mmmm.., it tastes really lovely.

Anyway, I can't help but think about life, you know, the ups and downs of it, the sweet and bitter moments, and the confusing bits too. I am right now reflecting on how far I have come in life and how much more lies ahead of me. I am cognisant of some of my human limitations in facing some of the challenges that life presents, and I am also thinking about the mistakes I have made thus far in life, the setbacks and disappointments I have had to deal with, and much, much more.

And so, this anthology you are about to hear or read is my reflections of some of the inspiring things I've learnt, and some of the things I wish I learnt earlier in my life. And it is also about being optimistic about life, and more importantly, it is a guide to being bold, strong, confident and courageous.

Let's get to it, shall we?

1. I have come to realise that every positive change in your life begins with a clear, unequivocal decision that you are either going to do something or stop doing something. Significant change starts when you decide to either get in or get out, either fish or cut the bait. The middle ground is very unstable and dangerous.

2. And as your life changes, your priorities also change. Certain things that were important at one stage in your life or career are no longer as important as you move to another stage of your life or to another level of responsibility. Therefore, it is wise to anticipate change and enlarge your capacity to adapt to the changing circumstances of life.

3. You must continuously ask yourself this; "what activities of my life can I cut back on, and which ones should I delegate or discontinue to free up more time for my most important activities. Remember, you only have 24 hours every day on which to do lots of things.
If you are very busy, you cannot effectively take on something new without deliberately deciding to discontinue something else, or effectively delegating. If you try to juggle lots of things, you will produce mediocre results. Therefore, choose your activities wisely and make sure you prioritise what matters most.

4. It is always best to be thoughtful, decisive, and action oriented.

5. Being decisive is one of the most important qualities of happy and successful men and women. And once a decision is made, it is important that appropriate action(s) is taken to materialise the object of the decision. Decisiveness and being action oriented are developed through practice and repetition – over, and over again until they become as natural as breathing in and out.

6. However, don't rush your decisions and actions. A wise man once said; "only fools rush in". Be patient but prudent. Weigh the options (by thinking them over) and choose the most potent one.

7. And, that leads me to also say that be honest in your dealings.

8. You see, a sincere and honest effort is nothing to be ashamed of. In the end, people appreciate frankness more than flattery.

9. That said, however, frankness is not a license to say anything you want, wherever and whenever you want to. Be careful about appearing rude in your attempt to be honest. The Bible tells us that there is a right time and a right way to do everything. Even if what you want to say is true, say it at the right time, and at the right tone, say it lovingly. Be sensitive to other people's feelings. Thoughtless words, though sincere and honest, often leave lasting wounds.

10. Unite truth with humility, for truth without humility is blind, and that's why it becomes contentious - it tries to support itself on something and finds nothing except rancour. Control your desire to just blurt out whatever your heart has 'cooked up'. Think through it first. Words matter, and how you say them, matters even more.

11. Live in harmony with each other. Don't try to act important, but rather enjoy the company of ordinary people. And don't think you know it all, or are a master of anybody. Just be a master of yourself.

12. And when arguments ensue, there is only one way under high heaven to get the best of an argument, do you know what it is? Avoid it. Yes, that's right, avoid arguments like you would avoid rattlesnakes and earthquakes. It is worth remembering that anyone convinced against their will are of the same opinion still. Arguing is so pointless, especially with someone who is intransigent and thinks they know it all or know it best (and that includes you sometimes). It is just best not to start an argument or get into one. Leave it alone and move on with what is important to you.

13. Moving on, always remind yourself regularly that your rewards will always be in direct proportion to your service to others. Jesus Christ rightly said; to be a master, you have to be a servant. Is that an oxymoron? No, not at all. It is so true that servanthood is the pathway to honour, a servant is welcome anywhere, and the real genius of true and humble servanthood is that it makes you a king at heart.

14. One of my favourite quotes is this: "Sharing is caring". O how true. I tell my children this quote whenever I have the opportunity to do so, and there is always an opportunity to do so, especially with the way children behave at times. When you genuinely care, you share. Sharing is indeed caring.

15. Caring is the basis of all purposes. It requires an openness to everything around you. To develop care, you need awareness, and you should not be burdened by a sense of duty or obligation. When you care naturally, it is because something has profoundly touched and moved you.

16. Let the heart within confess what the mouth utters; let the soul feel what the voice speaks. Live a life of purpose, Love God, love your neighbour and appreciate life. Care for one another. Choose to occupy your time and talents with people, commitments, ideas, and challenges that feel purposeful.

17. Finally, stop wasting time or being afraid, and start following your dreams. Think, decide and act, and follow your dreams. If not today, then when? If not you, then who? Time is ticking.

Let me end by saying this; be watchful, be thoughtful, be resourceful, and resolute. It is not enough to know what to do to make a positive difference in your life or other people's; the important thing is for you to do what you know is the right thing to do. Your readiness and effort are all that are needed. If you should fail ten times, do not be disheartened; if you should fail a hundred times, rise and pursue your way; if you should fail a thousand times, do not despair. When the right path is entered, success is sure if the path is not utterly abandoned.

I hope you know this by now about life; first strife, and then victory. First labour, and then rest. First weakness, and then strength. In the beginning the lower life, and the glare and confusion of battle, and then the Beautiful life, the Silence, and the Peace.

Stand tall, square your shoulders, lift your head, chin up, take a deep breath, and make a declaration that you are born free, and that you will exercise your inalienable right to chart the course of your life and follow your dreams.

Carpe diem, seize the moment.

Blessings to you.

Are you walking the path of Greatness?

No.	Question to consider	Tick
1	*Are you in control of your life?*	☐
2	*Are you more productive in your life?*	☐
3	*Are you rising to the top in your life?*	☐
4	*Are you focused in life?*	☐
5	*Are you financially free or on your way there?*	☐
6	*Are you influential?*	☐
7	*Have you unconditionally accepted yourself?*	☐
8	*Do you know who you are, and what your purpose is?*	☐
9	*Do you have great relationships?*	☐
10	*Have you risen above your mistakes, setbacks, and disappointments in life?*	☐
11	*Do you cope well with change in your life?*	☐
12	*Do you have mentors or advisors in your life?*	☐
13	*Do you deal well with emotional overwhelm?*	☐
14	*Are you happy?*	☐
15	*Do you know how to ask and get what you want?*	☐
16	*Are you clear about what you want in life?*	☐
17	*Have you mastered yourself yet?*	☐
18	*Are you self-controlled in your sexual habits?*	☐
19	*Do you stand guard at the door of your mind?*	☐
20	*Do you apply the ONE ESSENTIAL life principle in all you do?*	☐
21	*Have you stopped taking things for granted?*	☐
22	*Do you take time to reflect on your life?*	☐

> *Your life gets better when you get better. And since there is no limit on how much better you can become, there is also no limit on how much better your life can be. It is good to know that that is how it is.*
>
> *It is up to you to decide how much better you want your life to be.*

Afterword and Conclusion

If truth be told, it matters what we do with our lives here on earth, does it not?

For some people, they don't really care what they do, as long as they are enjoying themselves at the present moment. The future? Well, that will take care of itself, they say.

On the other hand, some people are genuinely concerned and worried about the state of affairs in the world, the environment, their health, their children etc, and they would very much want to do something about it NOW! Either way, your future is coming whether that be in a few minutes from now, tomorrow, next week, next month, next year or whenever it is; one thing is for sure, what you are doing right now with your life will contribute to what you will experience in that future.

Let me put it this way; your today was your future a few moments, days, weeks, months or years ago and whatever you are experiencing today is as a result of the decisions and actions you took back then. And your decisions and actions today will contribute to the kind of life you will live in the future. Not really complicated, is it? No.

Abuse your body today for example, and tomorrow you end up spending time in hospitals and visiting doctors to sort out your health.

Abuse the trust given to you today and tomorrow you lose the opportunity or privilege to serve in a special capacity.

Commit a crime today, and tomorrow you find yourself, where?..., Yes, that's right, in jail.

It all matters. What you do, how you do it, when you do it, where you do it from, and whom you do it with. It all matters, all of it. It is, therefore, important that you take care to be mindful of your decisions and actions because they have a huge impact on your life, now and in the future.

Succeeding in life and walking the path of Greatness purposefully every day doesn't come by chance. You have to put a concerted effort to ensure that what you desire to happen in your life is orchestrated with due care and attention.

What I have given you in this book, are insights, strategies and confidence building tips to help you live a successfully authentic, powerful, and great life in your own right. I am only a messenger, passing onto you what I, myself received, and I do so with love and with a sense of awe. What you do with it is up to you, but I hope you will use it to better yourself and the world around you.

I leave you with this quote by Walt Disney: "*All our dreams can come true - if we have the courage to pursue them.*"

Peace & Love to you.

About the Author

Sterling lives in London England with his family. He is a qualified Chartered Accountant, and besides helping business owners and entrepreneurs make sense of their numbers, Sterling spends most of his time encouraging and inspiring the people he interacts with to be the best versions of themselves, encouraging them to walk in the path of their own unique greatness, living lives of purpose, impact and influence.

Sterling believes that one of the most valuable gifts you can give yourself is that of being true yourself, being authentically you and living your life the best way you can without pretending to be someone else or trying to please everybody in order to fit in or be accepted by others. He is passionate about helping people to Discover, Develop and Deploy their gifts and talents for the betterment of themselves, and for the good of humanity.

He further encourages his listeners and audiences to dare to imagine great things for themselves, and keep the faith. Being Successful in life comes at a price - hard work, commitment, and relentlessness. And it is no guarantee that you can continue manifesting wealth and success if you rest on your laurels. That's why Sterling's view is that you have to keep doing the right things and redouble your efforts every so often.

Sterling lives his life by the following five principles:

1. Dare to dream big dreams and go after them.
2. Be true to yourself, be authentically you and grow.
3. Be decisive in life, and have goals.
4. Be open to all things but attached to nothing.
5. Do to others what you would have them do to you, and always do your best in life.

And here is Sterling's philosophy of life in three bullet points:

- You are not what you do or what you look like. A mistake many people make in life is to identify themselves with what they do or look like, and when that image is tampered with or altered by life circumstances, all sorts of problems ensue.

  Seeing through what you do or look like, to the essence of who you really are – a child of God, created in His image and likeness, a formless, boundless awareness, is the key to freedom, peace and power.

- And regardless of your physical address, your dominant state of consciousness or awareness is where you really live, it's your place of abode and everything you do, is from that place, and is affected by that place.

- **Think, Decide and Act**, and believe that you can have anything you want. Believe it with every part of your being, and nothing will stand in your way. All things are possible to those who believe. Jesus Christ said so.

To have Sterling Libs speak to your organisation, club, or community about the principles and strategies found in this book or success and productivity insights and principles, email sterlinglibs@gmail.com and for more information about Sterling, visit: www.sterlinglibs.com

Other books by S.G Libs

LIVING YOUR LIFE SUCCESSFULLY

The Ultimate Success Planning System for Super Achievers

This an amazing Success Planning System, a new kind of planner, journal and diary (three in one) that can help you set yourself up for success in whatever you do to realise your dreams. You will be able to achieve your goals in record time without stressing yourself out. It is for every serious person who needs to get more done faster but cannot figure out how to do so effectively. It is designed with high productivity in mind, and it will help you to achieve amazing success in your life.

What to expect

- ✓ **FAST RESULTS**! The High impact productivity action planner lets you achieve over ten times more than the average person in whatever you set out to do like *pro confident people do.*
- ✓ **BREAKTHROUGH!** Being purpose-driven and focused will help you stop wasting time doing things that don't work – *Immediately.*

- ✓ **EXCLUSIVE!** The Financial intelligence Money section makes it easier to plan to get all the money you dream of having - however much. ... *pragmatically and intelligently.*
- ✓ **A FRESH APPROACH**! The To-do list for Maximum Productivity, helps to clear your mind and bring structure to your day – *With Ease.*
- ✓ **OUTSTANDING!** The words of encouragement and inspiration ensure you can feel confident that you can accomplish whatever you set your mind to do and achieve great success at it. – *Quickly*
- ✓ **DEPENDABLE!** The Personal Development section helps you to become an unstoppable success as you daily develop yourself and hone your skills... *faster and easier than ever before.*
- ✓ **SUPERIOR PERFORMANCE!** The weekly review ensures you can develop the power to clarify your thinking and drive better decision making. ... *it has never been easier.*

So, if you want to supercharge your progress and make your efforts in life count for something worthwhile, then, **"LIVING YOUR LIFE SUCCESSFULLY"** is the answer you have been looking for! It is the most important Planner, Journal and Diary you will ever purchase! All in one.